# REVISION GUIDE

# OCR

INFORMATION and COMMUNICATION TECHNOLOGY for **AS**

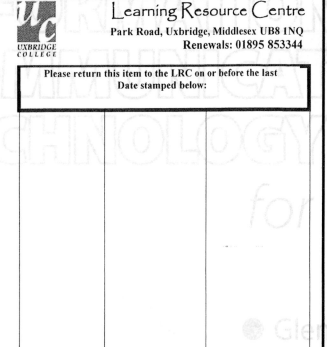
Glen Millbery
Sonia Stuart

HODDER
EDUCATION
AN HACHETTE UK COMPANY

The Publishers would like to thank the following for permission to reproduce copyright material:

**Photo credits**
**Running head image** © John Foxx/Imagestate Media; **p.7** © Mark Gabrenya/Shutterstock; **p.10** *TL* © Liette Parent/Fotolia; *TR* © Eric Isselée/Fotolia; *B* © Leonid Dorfman/Fotolia; **p.14** GreenGate Publishing Services; **p.30** *TL* © Miroslav Tolimir/istock; *TC* © Dinostock/Fotolia; *TR* © Anthony Hall/Fotolia; *ML* © LiquidImage/Fotolia; *MC* © Dragan Radojkovic/Fotolia; *MR* © Graça Victoria/Fotolia; *BL* © Alysta/Fotolia; *BR* © Experimental/Fotolia; **p.33** *TL* © Realistic Reflections/Getty Images; *M* © Picture Contact/Alamy; **p.35** © Rebecca Ellis/istock; **p.38** © Tony French/Alamy; **p.39** © John Tomaselli/Fotolia; **p.50** © Milos Jokic/Shutterstock; **p.78** © Sean O'Riordan/istock; **p.86** © Picture Contact/Alamy; **p.88** © Aleksandar Radovanovic/ Fotolia

**Acknowledgements**
Microsoft product screenshots reprinted with permission from Microsoft Corporation; **p.28** Linux Penquin logo reproduced with permission of Larry Ewing, lewing@isc.tamu.edu; **p.32** Photo of Braille keyboard reproduced with permission of Hooleon Keyboards, www. hooleon.com; **p.32** Photos of Braille printer and output reproduced with permission of Tech Ready, www.techready.co.uk; **p.33** Photo of tongue-activated joystick reproduced with permission of Compusult, www.compusult.net; **p.33** Photo of foot mouse reproduced with permission of Hunter Digital, www.footmouse.com; **p.46** Logos reproduced with permission of BP plc and Oxfam

Every effort has been made to trace all copyright holders, but if any have been inadvertently overlooked the Publishers will be pleased to make the necessary arrangements at the first opportunity.

Although every effort has been made to ensure that website addresses are correct at time of going to press, Hodder Education cannot be held responsible for the content of any website mentioned in this book. It is sometimes possible to find a relocated web page by typing in the address of the home page for a website in the URL window of your browser.

Hachette UK's policy is to use papers that are natural, renewable and recyclable products and made from wood grown in sustainable forests. The logging and manufacturing processes are expected to conform to the environmental regulations of the country of origin.

Orders: please contact Bookpoint Ltd, 130 Milton Park, Abingdon, Oxon OX14 4SB. Telephone: (44) 01235 827720. Fax: (44) 01235 400454. Lines are open 9.00–5.00, Monday to Saturday, with a 24-hour message answering service. Visit our website at www.hoddereducation.co.uk

© Glen Millbery, Sonia Stuart 2009

First published in 2009 by

Hodder Education,

An Hachette UK Company

338 Euston Road

London NW1 3BH

Impression number   5  4  3

Year                          2014

Cover photo © Ingram Publishing Limited

Illustrations by GreenGate Publishing Services

Typeset in ITC Stone Sans Medium 11pt by GreenGate Publishing Services, Tonbridge, Kent

Printed in Spain by GraphyCems

A catalogue record for this title is available from the British Library

ISBN: 978 1444 110937

# Contents

# Introduction

This book is not intended to be a text book that is used in class but is a revision guide that helps you prepare for your exam. It is a basic summary of the main points on which you will be assessed. It should be supplemented by notes that you make in class.

The revision guide follows the specification – each section contains a reference to the specification. The content is covered in either single pages or double-page spreads. To make life easier for you, all double-page spreads have been laid out on facing pages – this has sometimes meant that the lettering does not follow exactly the same order as the specification.

The revision guide is laid out with useful tips at the start of sections – these are things to look out for when answering questions on the topic. It has definitions and useful web links if you want to investigate a different aspect of the topic. The content itself has been reduced to the key points you need to know. However, this is a revision guide and although it tries to cover everything, it should be regarded as a supplement to your learning of the course.

There are questions at the end of each section and some items that you need to consider before answering questions on the topics covered. The questions are there to make you think about how the content will be applied in the examination. There are, of course, many other different questions you might be asked – these are not the only ones.

## 1.1 Data

**Specification reference**

**3.1.1a** – describe the term data, using an example, clearly identifying the fact that data has no meaning.

### Key points to remember

- Data is meaningless.
- Data is a collection of random characters.
- Data consists of raw facts before they have been processed.

### Data and information

**Keywords**

**Data:** a collection of **alphanumeric characters** without meaning.

**Alphanumeric characters:** numbers, letters or symbols.

**Weblink**

http://www.systems-thinking.org/dikw/dikw.htm

An explanation of the differences between data, information and knowledge.

**Data** is a big part of our lives – anything that is written or spoken is made up of data. Data is the raw facts and figures before they have been processed. 'Raw facts and figures' means facts and figures without meaning. It should not be possible to understand what the letters and figures stand for. For example:

090909     FDKA021.3

These are examples of data. There is no way to tell what they mean – they are just a random series of numbers and letters. To explain what they mean requires turning them into information.

### Exam questions

**1** Identify **two** characteristics of data.                [*2 marks*]

**2** Identify **two** pieces of data used in a hotel room booking system.                [*2 marks*]

### Examiner hints and tips

Think about the following in relation to the above questions.

**Question 1:** This is a learnt response – make sure that the two responses are different and do not cover the same point.

**Question 2:** You need to give random data. If you expand on what you have given to add meaning then it is no longer data. Make sure you give only two pieces of data and no context or structure.

## 1.2  Information

### Specification reference

**3.1.1b** – describe what is meant by the term information, using an example to show how data can become information through the use of context, structure and meaning.

### Key points to remember

- Information is processed data.
- Information means something.
- All examples given must use the context of the question.

## ■ Turning data into information

### Keywords

**Information:** data + context + structure + meaning.

**Context:** taking the data and giving it an environment where our prior knowledge and understanding can make sense of it.

**Structure:** the presentation of data, including any formatting.

**Meaning:** an understanding of what the data relates to.

**Information** is made by taking the data and processing it. Processing is performing some action on the data. This might be sorting, searching or editing.

Information = Data + [Context] + [Structure] + Meaning

In some cases, the data (raw facts and figures) does not need to have a context and a structure in order to become information. However, it is always best to know the complete formula and learn an example that has both structure and context. For example:

| Data | Context | Structure | Meaning |
|------|---------|-----------|---------|
| 14123 | UK £ | nnn.nn | £141.23 Amount in bank |
| –1286 | Fahrenheit | –nnn.n | –128.6 Coldest temperature recorded in Antarctica |

**Data in the form of binary coding**

## Exam questions

**1** Using an example related to pupils, show how data can become information. *[4 marks]*

**2** Using an example, describe what is meant by context and structure. *[4 marks]*

### Examiner hints and tips

Think about the following in relation to the above questions.

**Question 1:** You need to show how context and structure are added to data to give meaning. Stating the formula alone is not enough. You must use an example to obtain full marks.

**Question 2:** Again, an example must be given. It must be specific and show the data prior to context and structure being added. You must also explain what structure and context are and how they have changed the interpretation of the data.

## 1.3 Representation methods

### Specification reference

**3.1.1c** – describe different methods used to convey information: text, pictures, videos, animation, sound and LED, and give advantages, disadvantages and examples of the use of each.

### Keywords

**Text:** alphanumeric characters put together to deliver a message.

**Graphic:** picture, image or drawing.

**Sound:** a range of frequencies which can be used to transmit information.

**Video:** the technology of electronically capturing, recording, processing, storing, transmitting, and reconstructing a sequence of still images representing scenes in motion.

**LED:** a single point of light; LEDs can be grouped together to form multiple points.

### Weblink

**http://www.improvetheweb.com/use-text-instead-graphics-your-website**

Discussion of using text versus graphics on a website.

### Key points to remember

■ There are advantages and disadvantages of all representation methods.

■ The key methods to focus on are text, graphics, sound, moving pictures (animation or video) and light-emitting diode (LED).

## ■ Advantages and disadvantages

The main advantages and disadvantages of each representation method are shown in the table below:

| Method | Advantages | Disadvantages |
|---|---|---|
| Text | ■ Clear to understand<br>■ Lots of detail | ■ Need to be able to read<br>■ Need to understand the language<br>■ Lots of text cannot be read quickly<br>■ Directional |
| Graphics | ■ Do not need language to understand an image<br><br>■ Can match what you see | ■ Can be confusing if you do not understand the symbols used<br><br>■ Directional |
| Sound | ■ No fixed position<br>■ No line of sight required<br>■ Good for visually impaired people | ■ No good in large areas – distortion of sound<br>■ Usually language based<br>■ May not know the sound – e.g. different alarms have different sounds<br>■ Need to be able to hear |
| Moving pictures | ■ Lots of information conveyed<br>■ Not language dependent<br>■ Can exemplify text | ■ Linear – if you do not see the beginning you may not understand<br>■ Problems if sound |
| LED | ■ Can allow data to be kept secure<br>■ Can be used in noisy places<br>■ Similar to graphics | ■ Directional<br>■ Combinations of lights may need to be known to be understood |

## ■ Text versus graphics

There are overhead electricity cables ahead and the maximum height of a vehicle that will be able to pass safely under the cable is 16′ 6″

# Use of representation methods – considerations

When selecting an appropriate representation method to use, there are some criteria that can be used.

- **Language** – must the audience be able to understand a specific language?
- **Cultural** – are there cultural differences that may mean that the words or signs have different meanings?
- **Visibility** – can the audience see information from where they are or are there line of sight issues?
- **Complexity of information** – a picture is worth a thousand words but sometimes text can give more information.
- **Attention** – will the audience know the message has been given?
- **Physical disability** – sight/hearing problems are an issue in transferring information to an audience.

## Exam questions

**1** Using examples, describe **one** advantage and **one** disadvantage of using sound to convey a message to the crowd in an athletics stadium. [4 marks]

**2** Describe **two** advantages of using LED to convey information to people in a cinema. [4 marks]

## Examiner hints and tips

Think about the following in relation to the above questions.

**Question 1:** This is asking for an advantage and disadvantage of the same method for the given context. The response must give an example that demonstrates the advantage and disadvantage within the context of an athletics stadium.

**Question 2:** This is very specific – why LED should be used in a cinema. LED can be a single point of light or when combined can be used to create text.

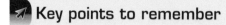

 **1.4**

# Knowledge

### Specification reference

**3.1.1d** – describe what is meant by the term knowledge, distinguishing the difference between information and knowledge.

 **Keywords**

**Knowledge:** application of information (to a given context) resulting in understanding.

**Application:** using information within a given context.

### Weblink

**http://www.nwlink.com/~Donclark/ history_knowledge/ knowledgehistory.html**

A brief history of information and knowledge.

## Key points to remember

- Knowledge is the application of information.
- Knowledge is the action that you need to take or a general rule you can determine from the information.

## ■ Creating knowledge

Data and information underpin **knowledge**. You cannot have knowledge without them. In the same way that information is built from data, so knowledge is built from information.

Statement 1: All cats have four legs

Statement 2: The animal in front of me has four legs

Conclusion: The animal in front of me is a cat

Logically this conclusion may or may not be correct, but if we apply knowledge – our understanding and perception of the world – we can tell whether it is a cat or not. The **application** of information to the context is knowledge.

All licensed London taxi drivers have to pass 'The Knowledge'. It is called this because it is more than information. It is the application of information – for example, routes, landmarks, road closures, etc.

# Converting information into knowledge

| Data | Information | Knowledge |
|------|-------------|-----------|
| 260 | Points needed in History, Economics and ICT to go to university | Can obtain BBD, CCC or ABE |
| 32 212 | Freezing and boiling point of water | 0 and 100 is celsius so must be referring to fahrenheit |

Information is based on certainties. Certainties are things that will occur the same way every time, or mean the same thing every time. They do not change or alter for a specific event.

In contrast, knowledge can change. It does not mean that every time it will change, but it can change. More information can be added to our knowledge and as we add more information we revise our knowledge.

For example, the boiling point of water changes with altitude.

## Exam questions

1 Using an example of information and an example of knowledge, describe the difference between information and knowledge. [*4 marks*]

2 Using examples, describe **two** characteristics of knowledge. [*4 marks*]

## Examiner hints and tips

Think about the following in relation to the above questions.

**Question 1:** This is asking for an example of information and an example of knowledge (1 mark for each) and the difference between the two (2 marks). Make sure the examples are relevant and are actual examples of information and knowledge – it is very easy to give two information examples.

**Question 2:** Again, this must be based on examples. The main characteristics are lack of certainty and application of information.

## 1.5 Data types

**Specification reference**

**3.1.1e** – describe different data types: Boolean, real, integer, string, date/time, selecting an appropriate data type for a given situation.

### 🔑 Keyword

**Data type:** defines the type of information that can be stored. For example, dates, numbers or characters.

### Weblink

**http://www.databasedev.co.uk/ fields_datatypes.html**

Data types in Microsoft Access.

### ⚡ Key points to remember

- The only data types you will be asked about are Boolean, real, integer, string, date/time.
- A telephone number is NOT a number.

## ■ Data types

There are only five **data types** that you need to be aware of:

| Data type | Definition | Example |
|-----------|-----------|---------|
| Boolean | One of only two values | True or false |
| Real | Numbers with decimals | 47.65 |
| Integer | Whole numbers | 43 |
| String | Alphanumeric characters | Hello World |
| Date/time | Numbers and letters | 07/06/1960 |

For a given situation you will need to use an appropriate data type. For example:

- **Currency:** Real because it can hold decimals
- **House number:** String because house numbers can contain letters – for example, 3c
- **Telephone number:** String because it has a leading 0 and spaces
- **Gender:** Boolean because there is a choice of two, i.e. male or female
- **Birthday:** Date so it can be calculated and be up to date

## Exam questions

**1** Identify the most appropriate data type for garden length and house price.   [*2 marks*]

**2** What is the difference between an integer and a real number?   [*2 marks*]

### Examiner hints and tips

Think about the following in relation to the questions opposite.

**Question 1:** This requires application and an understanding of the different scenarios. House price should not immediately give rise to a real number especially as large numbers are being dealt with.

**Question 2:** This is easy to get the wrong way round and needs to be learnt.

 **1.6** **Static and dynamic data**

**3.1.1g** – describe the terms static and dynamic data and compare the use of static information sources (for example, CD-ROM) with dynamic sources (for example, the internet).

 **Keywords**

**Static data:** data that remains the same after a refresh.

**Dynamic data:** data that can (but does not have to) change after a refresh.

### Weblink

**http://www.heathrowairport.com/ portal/page/Heathrow^General^ Flight+information^Live+flight+ arrivals/**

Examples of static and dynamic data.

 Key points to remember

- Static data does not change.
- Dynamic data can change.
- The two data types can be mixed together – for example, on a website.

| CD-ROM/magazines | The internet |
| --- | --- |
| There is a limited amount of information available | The internet has a large volume of information |
| Does not require access to the internet | Only people with internet access can access the data |
| More reliable source of information | The information is not always reliable |
| Need the CD/magazine | Can access through mobile phone/PDA |
| Data cannot be updated very quickly | Data can be updated very quickly |
| The CD can be scratched/broken or the magazine and CD lost/stolen | The internet might not be working. Difficulty accessing the pages |
| If there are errors, erratum notices would have to be sent out to people | The internet has many different opinions |
| Have to collect/wait for the magazine/CD | Available all the time from anywhere |
| Magazine does not have sound/ multimedia | Internet has a range of multimedia |

## Exam questions

**1** Compare a paper brochure with the internet for finding a holiday. [3 marks]

**2** Describe **two** advantages of using a CD instead of the internet for researching a project on the Normans. [4 marks]

### Examiner hints and tips

Think about the following in relation to the above questions.

**Question 1:** For 3 marks, you should give three comparisons. Each comparison should be on a different point and give both sides.

**Question 2:** The historical nature of the project is deliberate as it is unlikely that up to date information is required.

## 1.7 Data sources

**Specification reference**

**3.1.1f** – give examples of different sources from which data can be derived, for example gathered from original source or gathered from an indirect source, and explain the advantages and disadvantages of using each source.

### Key points to remember

- Direct data means no boundary exists between you and the data
- Indirect data has two meanings – a) someone else collects the data or b) the data is processed for a different purpose from which it was collected.

Data has to come from somewhere – it does not just appear. If you need some data, you must consider where to get it from.

If you have been given the task of creating a leaflet for a local cinema, you will need to find some data to go into the leaflet.

Where this data comes from is known as the source.

### Keywords

**Direct:** no one or thing comes between the source of the data and yourself when collecting the data.

**Indirect:** something comes between yourself and the data collection – it might be bought, another person collects it or it is collected for a different purpose.

Prepare for *your* exam...

REVISION GUIDE

OCR INFORMATION AND COMMUNICATION TECHNOLOGY AS

**Out now**

### Weblinks

**http://brent.tvu.ac.uk/dissguide/hm1u3/hm1u3text3.htm**

Different methods of collecting direct data.

**http://brent.tvu.ac.uk/dissguide/hm1u3/hm1u3text2.htm**

Different methods of collecting indirect data.

There are two sources – original (**direct**) and **indirect**. It is easiest to think of direct data as data that has been physically collected by you. This may be by questionnaire, interview, physically viewing or collecting the data.

Indirect data has two interpretations:

- Data that has been used for a purpose different to that for which it was originally collected. For example, collecting data on how many tickets have been sold for a film to make sure it is not oversold, and then using the data to find the most popular film.

- The people/companies involved in collecting the data are different to those using the data. Typically this might be organisations that conduct market surveys and then sell the results to other companies who use it in advertising.

## Advantages and disadvantages

| | Advantages | Disadvantages |
|---|---|---|
| Direct | ■ The source and collection method is known and verified.<br>■ The exact data required can be collected.<br>■ Can change the data being collected in response to answers. | ■ May not get a large range of data.<br>■ Data may not be available – location/time. |
| Indirect | ■ Large range of data available.<br>■ Data can be available from different locations and time periods.<br>■ Analysis might already have been completed on some of the data. | ■ Do not know if any bias was placed on the collection.<br>■ Cannot be certain of accuracy of the recording of data.<br>■ May not have all the information about how, when and where it was collected to make a valued opinion on its usefulness. |

## Exam questions

1 Describe **two** advantages to using direct data sources to collect information on how good a new paperback book by your favourite author is. [4 marks]

2 Describe **two** advantages of using indirect data sources to collect information on airplane passenger numbers. [4 marks]

## Examiner hints and tips

Think about the following in relation to the above questions.

**Question 1:** This is a very specific scenario and it focuses on the advantages of you collecting the information rather than getting it from an indirect source.

**Question 2:** This is looking for answers relating to time and volume.

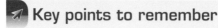

 **1.8** # Quality of information

## Specification reference

**3.1.1h –** describe how the following can affect the quality of the information produced: accuracy, relevance, age, completeness, presentation, level of detail.

### Keyword

**Quality of information:** how useful that information is in the target area for which it has been produced – how easy it is to turn it into the required knowledge.

### Weblink

**http://www.virtualchase.com/ quality/**

Evaluating the quality of information on the Internet.

### ⚡ Key points to remember

■ Examples must be contextualised.

■ Do not repeat the key word when describing it – use other words.

## Accuracy

The information needs to be correct. If it is not accurate you cannot rely on it. If you are asked what day the concert is on and you give the wrong day, people will miss it.

## Relevance

The information must relate to the topic. Having information that is not relevant increases the volume of data and can take time to look at. If you asked who was playing at the concert and were told that the concert is on Monday it is not useful or relevant information.

## Age

Information from the past may not be relevant today. Age can affect the accuracy of information. For example, asking where the concert is and being told that last year it was at Wembley.

## Completeness

This is only having some of the information. For example, asking when the concert is and being given a date but no time.

## Presentation

This is how easy it is to extract the information from. This is related to format and layout – for example, a page of text telling you the train times instead of a table.

## Level of detail

The volume of information – too much or too little information. For example, directions that include every single turning can be too much information.

## Exam questions

**1** Using an example, demonstrate how accuracy, level of detail and completeness are linked. [*3 marks*]

**2** Describe, using examples, how the quality of information can be affected by its presentation. [*2 marks*]

### Examiner hints and tips

Think about the following in relation to the questions opposite.

**Question 1:** All three factors have connections. You will need an example to show those connections. The three factors are slightly different so it is important not to repeat yourself.

**Question 2:** This focuses on one aspect of the quality of information. Make sure the example has enough scope to give a full answer.

  **Encoding data**

## Specification reference

**3.1.1i** – describe the advantages and disadvantages of encoding data.

## ⤤ Key points to remember

■ Encoding is not the same as cryptography.

■ The aim of encoding is not to increase security.

## ■ Advantages and disadvantages of encoding data

### 🔑 Keyword

**Encoding:** transforming the data from one format into another. Can include shortening, symbol replacement or abbreviations.

### Weblink

**http://www.blooberry.com/ indexdot/html/topics/urlencoding. htm**

Encoding used for web URLs (Uniform Resource Locators).

### Example of encoding

| Month | Encoding |
| --- | --- |
| January | Jan |
| February | Feb |
| March | Mar |
| April | Apr |
| May | May |
| June | Jun |
| July | Jul |
| August | Aug |
| September | Sep |
| October | Oct |
| November | Nov |
| December | Dec |

| Advantages | Disadvantages |
| --- | --- |
| **Less memory requirement** Storing less information, therefore less memory is required. | **Precision of data coarsened** For example, Light Blue encoded as Blue. |
| **Security** If the codes are not apparent then it is difficult to know and understand the meaning of the codes. | **Encoding of value judgements** For example, 'Was the film good?' to be encoded as a judgement of 1–4. This will be encoded differently by different people and makes comparisons difficult. |
| **Speed of input** The codes take less time to enter, therefore it is quicker to input a large volume of data. | **The user needs to know the codes used** If the user does not know the codes they cannot use them. |
| **Data validation** Since the codes follow a strict set of numbers and letters they are easy to validate. | **Limited number of codes** If codes are made up of a range of letters and numbers the options will be limited. |
| **Organisation of data** If the data is in a standardised format then it can be compared and organised. | **Difficult to track errors** Validation will ensure the code is entered correctly but the nature of the code will make it difficult to see if the code is actually correct. |

## Exam questions

**1** Using an example, show how encoding can coarsen the precision of data. [*3 marks*]

**2** Describe **one** advantage of encoding data collected by a survey. [*2 marks*]

## Examiner hints and tips

Think about the following in relation to the above questions.

**Question 1:** You are given one of the disadvantages and need to use an example to demonstrate how it is a disadvantage.

**Question 2:** The context is a survey and this needs to be your focus. Speed of writing it down is the obvious advantage to choose.

## 1.10 Validation

 **Keywords**

**Range:** difference between upper and lower value.

**Type:** data type must match.

**Presence:** data must be entered.

**Length:** maximum and minimum characters entered.

**Picture:** follows predefined rules for each data type at each position.

**Check digit:** mathematically calculated check.

### Key points to remember

- Validation cannot ensure the accuracy of data entered.
- Validation ensures the data is reasonable, sensible and within the boundaries of predefined rules.

### ■ Definition

Validation is a check that is performed by the computer as the data is being entered. It tries to prevent entry of any data that does not conform to pre-set rules.

There are many different rules that can be created; however, they will not stop incorrect data being entered, they will just ensure that the data that is entered is:

- sensible
- reasonable
- within acceptable boundaries
- complete.

### Range checks

A range check sets an upper and a lower boundary for the data. The data entered must lie between these two values. For example, the price of a home printer must lie between 10 and 1000. Anything outside this range will be rejected.

### Type checks

This makes sure that the data entered is of the correct type. Types of data include: Numeric, String, Boolean and Date/Time.

### Presence checks

These are also called existence checks. Not every field or question would need to be answered. However, there will be some that must have an answer and be filled in.

### Length checks

When any data is entered into a computer it has a length. A single character has a length of 1, 'Hello' has a length of 5. Length checks ensure that the maximum and minimum length is achieved by the data entered.

## Lookup Validation

This looks up the data in another table to ensure that it is valid. It might also return additional information – entering the postcode and house number returns the rest of the address.

## Picture checks

This is also known as a format check. It checks the data type of each character in each position to check it conforms to rules.

## Check digit

A check digit is calculated using a set of numbers and then added to the end of them. When the code is created, the check digit is created and added to the code. Before the code is processed, the check digit is recalculated and compared with the one in the code. If they are the same, processing continues. If they are not, an error has occurred and the code value needs to be re-entered.

# ■ Validation and data types

Not all validation rules can be applied to all data types.

| Validation | Data types |
|---|---|
| Range | All data types |
| Type | Cannot be applied to string |
| Presence | All data types |
| Length | All data types |
| Picture | All data types |
| Check digit | Integer only |

More than one rule can be applied to the same field. For example, to validate a telephone number, the field must be a string (cannot be validated), so you could apply a presence check, length check and picture check.

## Exam questions

1 Give **three** examples of data that could be entered into a form, that are incorrect, but would pass **three** different validation rules. [3 marks]

2 Show how check digit validation can be applied to the ISBN 0-7487-9116-7 to show that it is a valid entry under Modulus 11. [4 marks]

## Examiner hints and tips

Think about the following in relation to the questions opposite.

**Question 1:** You need to give three different pieces of data and three different validation rules. This question is targeting the fact that validation cannot ensure accuracy.

**Question 2:** This requires an understanding of check digit validation. You are given the fact that it is an ISBN and the method of check digit validation. Show every step of the calculation.

# 1.11 Verification

## Specification reference

**3.1.1k** – describe and give examples of the following verification methods: double entry with automatic comparison and proof reading, and understand that verification does not ensure the data is correct but that it is entered correctly and reduces errors.

## ⚲ Key points to remember

- Verification cannot ensure the accuracy of data entered.
- Verification ensures the data is entered correctly, not that it is correct.

## ■ Definition

If you have collected some information on paper, at some point it will need to be entered into the computer.

Once you have entered it into the computer you will have two copies: the paper-based original and the copy stored in the computer.

- The paper-based copy is known as the source document.
- The copy in the computer is known as the object document.

### Keywords

**Computer verification:** data is entered twice and the computer performs the task of matching the two sets of data looking for mistakes.

**Manual verification:** the individual is responsible for making sure the object and source are the same – either the same person re-reading or another person reading both copies.

| Source | Data entry | Object |
|---|---|---|
| 75422 60992<br>26345 62561<br>92132 97090<br>55421 73392<br>61434 63474 |  | 7542260992<br>26345 62561<br>9213297090<br>5542173392<br>6143463474 |

### Weblink

**http://www.copyediting.co.uk/test. htm**

Proof reading test to try out.

Verification is making sure that the information on the source document is the same as the information on the object document.

Put simply it is making sure that the same information that is on the paper has been entered and not changed in any way – it is an exact copy.

It does not ensure that the information is correct.

There are two main methods of verification:

1 **Computer verification** (also known as double entry)

2 **Manual verification** (also known as proof reading)

The two main errors are transcription and transposition errors. Transcription is miscopied. Transposition is where numbers or letters are put round the wrong way.

# ■ Computer verification (double entry)

This involves entering the data twice (manually). The computer then compares the two sets of data and if it finds any differences it informs the user.

If there are any differences, then one of the entries is correct and the other is wrong. The user can then make the appropriate changes.

The double entry method can be used by the same person or different people.

The main problem with double entry is that if the same error is made both times then the computer will not find a difference.

# ■ Manual verification (proof reading)

This involves the entry on the paper being manually compared with the entry typed into the computer.

This relies on the person being able to follow two sets of data and find any differences. It is very difficult to transfer attention between paper and a screen. It is also difficult to keep track of where you are on the paper and where you are looking on the screen.

## Exam questions

**1** Using an example, show how verification cannot ensure that the data is correct. [*2 marks*]

**2** Give examples of transcription and transposition errors and show how they would be picked up by computer verification. [*4 marks*]

## Examiner hints and tips

Think about the following in relation to the above questions.

**Question 1:** You need to come up with an example and show that data is transferred incorrectly.

**Question 2:** This requires two examples and an understanding of computer verification to show how the errors would be picked up.

**1.12** # Back-up and archiving

 **Specification reference**

**3.1.1l** – explain the difference between backing up and archiving of data and give reasons why they are necessary.

 **Keyword**

**External media:** media that can be removed. For example, USB memory stick, external hard disk drive and internet back-up.

**Weblink**

http://www.freebsd.org/doc/en/books/handbook/backup-strategies.html

Back-up strategies.

## Key points to remember

- A back-up is a copy.
- Archiving is moving data, usually to an external source.

Back-up is keeping a copy of the current data. If there is a failure of the computer system (for example, a power failure leading to corruption, a virus, files being accidentally deleted, etc.), then the back-up can be used to restore the data.

Back-up is important so that data is not lost. Information is valuable and needs to be protected. Once created the back-up should not be stored in the same location – it should be on removable media and taken to another location.

Archiving is for long-term storage of data that is not required immediately. In fact, archived data is often not required at all. It is taken off the system and stored in case it is required for an investigation in the future. When archiving, data is written to a large capacity storage device at long intervals, unlike back-ups, which should be written at short intervals.

Files should be archived when they are no longer needed immediately, and when you don't want to delete them permanently. Examples of these types of files would be last year's financial or sales records, completed projects and details of former employees and old orders.

When you archive old files, you eliminate the waste of time and media that results from backing up unused files, free up hard drive space, and improve the performance of the system.

## Exam questions

**1** What is the difference between backing up and archiving of data? [3 marks]

**2** Describe **two** reasons why it is necessary to archive data. [4 marks]

### Examiner hints and tips

Think about the following in relation to the above questions.

**Question 1:** This is testing whether you know the correct definitions of archive and back-up and don't get them confused.

**Question 2:** This is a question that goes beyond the simple definition. Two reasons are required and they should be related to their advantages.

## 1.13 Costs of producing information

### Specification reference

**3.1.1m** – describe the costs of producing information in terms of hardware, software, consumables and personnel.

### Keywords

**Hardware:** a physical device, something that can be touched and seen.

**Software:** programs and code – cannot be physically seen or touched; only the results of running the software can be seen.

**Consumables:** paper, ink, toner, electricity.

**Personnel:** hiring, training and time.

### Weblink

http://www.teach-ict.com/ as_a2_ict_new/ocr/AS_G061/311_ data_info_knowledge/cost_of_ information/miniweb/index.htm

Teaching website on the costs of producing information.

### Key points to remember

■ The costs are of producing and not of delivering.

■ There are four main costs involved in producing information. Each of these can be sub-divided.

## Hardware

**Hardware** can be used to collect the information, process it and output it. It can also be used to store the information for use at a later date. It may be necessary for the organisation to purchase items of hardware. Ongoing hardware costs include repair and maintenance costs as well as upgrade costs.

## Software

**Software** needs to be purchased. In addition to the operating system this may include (depending on the context) DTP, graphics and website software.

## Consumables

**Consumables** are items that get used – paper, printer ink, toner and electricity being the main items.

## Personnel

**Personnel** costs are the costs related to people working in the organisation. People are required to collect, collate, enter, process and output information. There may also be costs involved in sending people on software training courses, and the associated costs of covering their jobs whilst they are absent. Depending on the information that is being produced, there may be additional costs that involve checking the accuracy of the data.

### Exam questions

1 Identify **two** hardware and **two** software costs, in addition to the standard computer, that will be incurred when producing a website. [4 marks]

2 Describe **two** personnel costs incurred by an organisation wanting to produce a leaflet. [4 marks]

### Examiner hints and tips

Think about the following in relation to the questions opposite.

**Question 1:** The hardware and software costs you give are in addition to the standard computer (mouse, keyboard, monitor, operating system, etc.). You will not get marks for those components/software.

**Question 2:** This is a straightforward description response and should focus on training, hiring/wages and temporary staff costs.

## 1.14 Input, processing, output, storage and feedback

### Specification reference

**3.1.1n** – describe clearly the terms input, processing, output, storage and feedback, drawing a diagram to illustrate how they are related.

### Keywords

**Input:** getting data external to the system into the system.

**Processing:** performing an action on the data. For example, edit, sort, save, etc.

**Output:** getting data that is within the system out of the system.

**Storage:** saving data for later use.

**Feedback:** taking the output and making it into the next cycle of input.

### Weblink

**http://hubpages.com/hub/How-computer-input--process-and-out-put-information**

How a computer inputs, processes and outputs information.

### Key points to remember

- You must know the ICT system block diagram, including the terms and direction of flow of data.
- You may be asked to draw the diagram, describe the terms or apply the terms and diagram to a given context.

## ■ Definitions

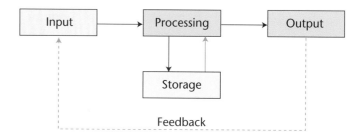

### Input

This is taking information that is external to the system and entering it into the system. This may be manual input (e.g. keyboard) or automated input (e.g. OMR). It may also be input by electronic means – via a network or CD/disk.

### Processing

This is an action performed on the data. Processing can include sorting, searching or performing calculations on the data.

### Output

This is taking information that was in the system and outputting it. The method used may result in printed output, screen output or electronic output (e.g. disk/CD).

### Storage

This is where data is held. It may be the data that has been input, data required during processing or the results of processing. This is data that is still within the system.

### Feedback

This is where the output from the system forms part of the input to the system. Feedback is usually applied to real-time situations. If the response to the feedback is automatic then the process is a closed loop. If there is an operator involved then the process is an open loop.

# ■ Applying the terms

You will need to know how to apply the ICT system block diagram to a context. The context will not be written using the key terms. You will need to work out which part of the process is which and then turn the text into a diagram.

## Example

Mike applies for a ticket to a concert. He is told that all tickets have been sold but he will be put on a waiting list in case of returns. If a ticket is returned then he will be notified and asked if he still wants to buy the ticket.

### Input

The initial ticket request from Mike.

The secondary feedback input if a ticket becomes available.

### Processing

Based on the initial request, searching to find a ticket.

Once a ticket is returned, searching to find people on the waiting list.

### Output

The initial response – 'no tickets available'.

The notification once a ticket becomes available.

### Storage

Storing ticket details.

Storing customer (Mike) details.

### Feedback

Having found Mike on the waiting list, asking if he still wants the ticket.

## Exam questions

1 Using a diagram, show how the terms input, processing, output, storage and feedback are related.    [4 marks]

2 Using the context of a heating system, use a diagram to show the input, storage, processing, output and feedback.    [4 marks]

## Examiner hints and tips

Think about the following in relation to the questions opposite.

**Question 1:** If you do not use a diagram you will not get any marks. This is the straightforward reproduction of the diagram.

**Question 2:** This also requires a diagram but the application of a context rather than the learnt response.

## 2.1 Difference between hardware and software

### Specification reference

**3.1.2a** – describe the difference between hardware and software, giving examples of each to illustrate the description and explain the lack of standardisation affecting both hardware and software.

### Keywords

**Hardware:** a physical device, something that can be touched and seen.

**Software:** programs and code – cannot be physically seen or touched; only the results of running the software can be seen.

### Weblink

**http://www.compinfo-center.com/tpstan-t.htm**

Directory of computer standards.

### Key points to remember

- Hardware is physical, software is programs.
- Standardisation is about how data can be exchanged.

**Hardware** is the physical components that make up a computer system – the items you can touch, such as monitor, keyboard and mouse.

**Software** is the programming code required to run programs on the computer. This includes the operating system, applications software and utilities.

## ■ Standardisation

Standardisation is about enabling one piece of hardware to work with another and enabling data to be transferred from one package to another.

If you have two different systems there might be incompatibility in the hardware and software. This can have the following negative impacts:

- No communication between systems/miscommunication between systems leading to incorrect data being passed.
- New equipment having to be purchased to bridge the gap.
- The cost of training staff on the systems.
- Lack of technical support on the systems.

## Exam questions

**1** Using examples, describe the difference between hardware and software. [*4 marks*]

**2** Describe **two** problems that could be caused by a lack of hardware standardisation. [*4 marks*]

### Examiner hints and tips

Think about the following in relation to the questions opposite.

**Question 1:** There are 4 marks, 2 for the examples and 2 for the difference. You need to include one characteristic of hardware and a different one about software.

**Question 2:** The answers could focus on training, technical support or specific examples to do with data loss.

# 2.2 Specialist software devices

## Specification reference

**3.1.2d** – describe specialist software for physically disabled users: predictive text, sticky keys, zoom, voice recognition.

## Keywords

**Physically disabled:** any physical impairment that restricts the use of the computer. Can be motor impaired, visually impaired or auditory impaired.

**Specialist software:** software that has been written to assist the physically disabled.

### Weblink

**http://www.nytimes. com/2008/12/18/technology/18iht-18software.18792441.html**

Newspaper article on software for disabled users.

 **Key points to remember**

- Software is programs, no hardware answers can be given.
- The specialist software must be appropriate for the disability – physical, auditory or visual.

The most common **specialist software** aid for the visually impaired is a screen reader – a program that reads out a computer display. The screen reader may output information in Braille, use voice output, or use other audio signals to indicate graphics on the screen.

Other tools that can be useful include:

- Auditory feedback – this plays sounds in response to user activity, for example noises for key presses, opening windows and menus and deleting files. This is useful as it confirms the action.

- Screen magnifier – a utility that can zoom in on portions of the screen to make it easier to view information on computer monitors.

- Predictive text – this suggests the required word as the letters are typed so the user does not have to type the whole word.

- Sticky keys – these are useful for those people that find it difficult to hold down more than one key at a time. Sticky keys allow a key to be pressed once and the system to act as if it is was being continually pressed. It allows combinations involving the Ctrl, Alt or Shift keys, by pressing only one key at a time.

## Exam questions

**1** Describe **two** items of specialist software used by an employee who does not have the use of their arms. [4 marks]

**2** Explain how specialist software can improve how a visually impaired employee can use a computer. [4 marks]

## Examiner hints and tips

Think about the following in relation to the above questions.

**Question 1:** Not all items of specialist software are appropriate – this question narrows down the options.

**Question 2:** This is the application of software to a specific situation – the marks are not for identifying or describing, but how they are used.

## 2.3  Types of software

### Specification reference

**3.1.2e** – describe different types of software (operating systems, user interfaces, utilities, applications software) and give examples of how and where each type of software would be used.

### Keyword

**Software:** computer programs that provide the instructions that enable the computer hardware to work.

### Weblink

**http://computer.howstuffworks.com/operating-system.htm**

Describes how the operating system works.

**The logo of the Linux operating system**

**Example of a command line**

### Key points to remember

■ You must use generic software names and not proprietary names.

■ The examples of use of each type of software must be contextualised.

There are various types of **software**:

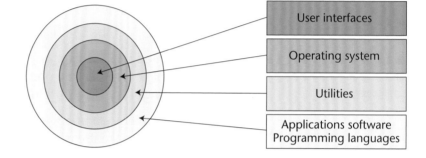

## ■ Operating system

The operating system controls the allocation and usage of hardware resources such as memory, central processing unit (CPU) time, hard disk space, and peripheral devices. It performs basic data management tasks such as recognising input from the keyboard, sending output to the display screen, and keeping track of files and directories on the hard disk.

Without the operating system the computer will not function.

## ■ User interfaces

The user interface is the means by which the user can interact with the application or operating system.

There are different types of user interface:

■ Menu – an on-screen list of options.

■ Form – an on-screen space for you to type.

■ Command line – a space to type instructions.

■ Natural language – a voice-based interface.

Their use will depend on the context – for example, command line for expert users, natural language in a quiet environment/for a disabled user, menu to give a list of selectable options and form to mirror paper.

### Weblink

**http://www.opensourcelist.org/oss/suggestedapplications.html**

Examples of open source applications.

# Utilities

**Utilities** are small programs that assist in the monitoring and maintaining of the computer system. There is a blurring between the boundaries of operating systems and utilities, with many utilities being bundled with operating systems.

Examples of utility programs include:

- Printer monitoring software
- Virus checkers
- File compression software.

# Applications software

These are programs that allow the computer to be used to solve particular tasks for the end user. Applications software includes programs such as:

- Word processors
- Spreadsheets
- Databases
- Communications (email)
- Graphics packages.

How they are used will vary according to the context.

**Examples of applications software**

## Exam questions

**1** Identify **two** different types of applications software an estate agent could use and give an example for the use of each.

[4 marks]

**2** Describe, using examples, the role of utility programs. [4 marks]

## Examiner hints and tips

Think about the following in relation to the above questions.

**Question 1:** Make sure you use generic names and not proprietary software names. Give the applications software name and then the contextualised use.

**Question 2:** This needs examples but the focus is on the role. Just describing two different utilities will not achieve full marks.

## 2.4 Input, output and storage devices

### Specification reference

**3.1.2b** – identify an appropriate input, output or storage device for a given situation and justify the choice made.

### Key points to remember

- Know the difference between an input and an output device.
- The context will be looking for a range of devices. It will also eliminate a range of devices. Make sure you read the scenario carefully.

### Keywords

**Input device:** a device that gets data external to the system into the system.

**Output device:** a device that gets data that is in the system out of the system.

### Weblink

http://electronic-components.
globalspec.com/productfinder/
electrical_electronic_components/
data_input_devices

Descriptions of different input devices.

## Input device

An **input device** is a piece of hardware that gets information into a computer. Examples include keyboard, concept keyboard, touch screen, microphone, scanner mouse and digital camera.

There are many different types of scanner, for example, bar code, magnetic and flatbed. You need to be specific when referring to scanners.

## Output device

An **output device** is a piece of hardware that gets information out of the computer and displays it to the end user. Examples include printers, speakers, monitors and LEDs.

There are many different types of printer, for example laser, inkjet and dot matrix. You need to be specific when referring to printers.

## Storage device

This is any device that stores data. Examples include ROM, RAM, hard drive, as well as portable devices such as external hard drive, CD-R/W, DVD-R/W and USB memory stick.

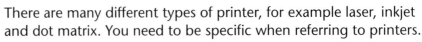

# ■ Applying the devices

The question will ask you to identify the most appropriate device within a given context.

You need to think about different things. All the ideas below relate to using specific devices as answers:

## Input

- Are there a fixed number of inputs or a range of inputs?
- Is the input pre-prepared/printed/on a strip, etc.?
- Does the input method require accuracy of movement?
- Context specific input devices – for example, a light beam on conveyor or a pressure pad for weighing luggage in airport.

## Output

- Is the output focused or widespread?
- What quality of output is required?
- Is there a data protection issue regarding the output?
- Speed of output.

## Storage

- Portability – how easy can it be carried around?
- Capacity – how much information can it hold?
- Cost – usually per MB.
- Speed of data transfer (linked to method of access – serial/direct).

You need to identify the device (make sure you give the device and not software) and a justification for its use.

## Exam questions

**1** Identify **two** input devices, apart from mouse and keyboard, that could be used in a shop and give an example of their use.
[4 marks]

**2** Justify **two** different situations where the use of a memory stick would be more appropriate than an internal hard drive.
[4 marks]

## Examiner hints and tips

Think about the following in relation to the questions opposite.

**Question 1:** You cannot use mouse or keyboard as an answer. You need to think of two other devices that you can give an appropriate example of use for.

**Question 2:** This is a slightly different way of phrasing the question – you are given the device and have to come up with two examples of use, justifying your answers against another given device.

### Specification reference

**3.1.2c** – describe specialist hardware devices for physically disabled users: puff-suck switch, foot mouse, eye typer, Braille printers and keyboards, speakers and microphones.

### 🔑 Keyword

**Visually impaired:** a loss of vision – it may be total loss of vision in one or both eyes (blindness) or partial loss.

### Weblink

**http://www.nfb.org/Images/nfb/ Publications/fr/fr21/fr06ws12.htm**

Examples of assistive technology for blind students.

### Key points to remember

- Different devices are suitable for different groups of people.
- These are hardware devices, NOT software.

There are two main groups of physically disabled who require special devices to use a computer – visually impaired and motor impaired. The hardware can be broken into input and output devices.

## ■ Visually impaired

Hardware devices that can assist the **visually impaired** include:

- Braille keyboard – a keyboard with Braille dots on the keys.

**Braille keyboard**

- Microphone – an input device for voice recognition.
- Loudspeaker – an output device for hearing signals and text read out.
- Screen magnifier (hardware not software) – a magnifying glass that fits on top of the screen and enlarges parts of it.
- Braille printer – an impact printer that can create Braille on a page.

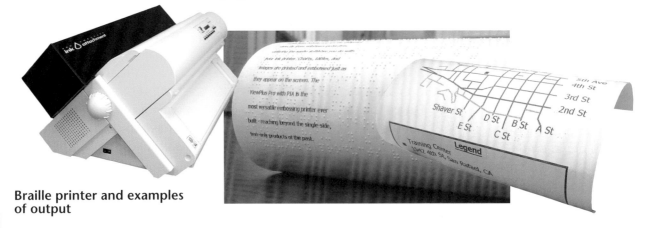

**Braille printer and examples of output**

# ■ Motor impairment

Hardware devices that can assist **motor impairment** include:

- Mouth stick – a stick for inputting controlled with the mouth.
- Puff-suck switch (or blow-suck tube) – a tube placed in the mouth and blown/sucked through.
- Tongue-activated joystick – placed in the mouth and manipulated with the tongue.

**Mouth stick**

**Tongue-activated joystick**

- Eye typer – a device that fits onto the muscles around the eye and when the eye is moved a pointer on the screen moves.
- Foot mouse – a mouse that is controlled by the foot.

**Eye typer**

## Exam questions

**1** Describe **two** specialist input devices that could be used by an employee who does not have the use of their arms. [*4 marks*]

**2** Describe how a physically disabled user could make use of an eye typer. [*2 marks*]

## Examiner hints and tips

Think about the following in relation to the above questions.

> **Question 1:** This is looking for devices that do not need the hands to be operated. An identification of the device and a description of its use is required.

> **Question 2:** This has given the device – eye typer – and you are required to give examples of its use.

**Foot mouse**

## 2.6 User interfaces

**Specification reference**

**3.1.2f** – describe the characteristics of different styles of user interface, command-based, forms, dialogue, natural language, WIMP interfaces (windows, icons, menus, pointers), and their appropriate uses.

### Key points to remember

- Although there is crossover between the types of interface, each has its own characteristics.
- The use of the interface is dependent on the context and scenario.

### Keywords

**User interface:** the method by which the user communicates with the computer.

**Characteristic of interface:** a feature or aspect that is central to the particular interface.

## ■ Command-based

This is where the user is presented with a command prompt. The commands are typed in to the computer.

If the interface is only command-based, it takes up less memory and this has the effect of running the commands faster. A large number of commands have switches. These are parameters added to the end of the main command which add functionality.

Command-based systems are for use by expert users with a good understanding of the commands they are using. They are useful for running commands which cannot be accessed from a menu or form.

## ■ Forms

A form is a limited area on screen with boxes to fill in. It has labels to help the user (for example, what data to input) and spaces to enter data. The latter might be drop down boxes, open text or option buttons.

Forms can guide the user through entering the relevant information in a structured manner. They can include the default options for the user and give context-based assistance. The data entry boxes can also be validated.

Another type of interface which makes use of forms is a dialogue interface. This asks questions and requires a response before continuing. Error messages that appear (and must be dealt with) are part of a dialogue interface.

Weblink

http://trillian.randomstuff.org.uk/~stephen/history/#wimp

History of the WIMP interface.

## ■ WIMP

WIMP (windows, icons, menus and pointers) is an interface that contains a rectangular area that can hold an application or icons. Icons are graphic symbols that denote a program, command, file or a concept. A menu is a series of related items that can be selected (see page 35). A pointer is an arrow on screen that mirrors the movement of the hand and can be used to select icons and windows.

# Menus

Menus are a series of related items that can be selected. Menus are either pop-up or pull-down. Menus can be structured – for example, the top word in a pull-down menu gives an indication of what the menu is about.

Menus can be cascaded, that is one menu leads to another menu. Items on menus can appear faded to show they cannot be used in a particular context.

Menus are useful where there is a limited set of commands that can be used in a specific situation. Each menu can have a keyboard shortcut which makes it work with a variety of input devices.

# Natural language

Natural language interfaces allow the users to use their own language to communicate with the computer. It does not require any specific commands.

There are two main types of natural language interface – spoken and written. Spoken interfaces are typified by voice recognition software which allows you to speak into a word processor. Written natural language interfaces include Microsoft Help and Ask. com. PDAs (Personal Digital Assistants) can include software that recognises handwriting.

## Exam questions

**1** Describe, using examples, the components of a WIMP interface. [*4 marks*]

**2** Identify **two** characteristics of a natural language interface and give an example of use. [*3 marks*]

### Examiner hints and tips

Think about the following in relation to the above questions.

**Question 1:** Go through the four components (windows, icons, menus and pointers) and give an example of use for each. Note that windows is not Microsoft Windows.

**Question 2:** You need to select the type of natural language that will form the basis of the answer – it has not been specified in the question.

# Characteristics of standard applications software and application areas

 **Standard/generic applications software**

 **Specification reference**

**3.1.3a** – identify basic tasks that standard/generic applications software can readily be used for: letter writing, memos, reports, flyers, brochures, posters, business cards, graphs, modelling, forecasting, data handling, sorting, searching, mail merging, web page authoring, presentations.

 **Key points to remember**

- Standard/generic applications software can be used to carry out a range of tasks.

- The software selected must be appropriate to the task being completed.

## Word processing

A word processor is a generic applications package that allows the entry, editing and formatting of text to create a range of documents. A user enters data using a keyboard or through the use of speech via a microphone. The text on the screen can then be formatted to meet the needs of the user, edited, saved and printed. Most word processing packages have **WYSIWYG** features.

Tasks that can be completed using WYSIWYG features include the creation of letters, memos and reports.

### Keywords

**Standard/generic applications software:** software that is provided for a range of tasks rather than one specific task, for example word processing or spreadsheet software.

**WYSIWYG:** what you see is what you get.

**Spreadsheet:** an application consisting of a table of rows and columns. Cells can contain labels, data or formulae that enable automatic calculations to be carried out.

## Desktop publishing

Desktop publishing (DTP) packages allow users to combine images and text to create publications. A DTP package focuses on the manipulation and accurate positioning of graphical objects on the page, including text, to create a composite publication.

Tasks that can be completed using DTP packages include the creation of flyers, posters, brochures and business cards.

## Database

Database packages enable a user to handle data. The data can be split into tables and relationships created between the tables to allow the data to be joined together. The data can be sorted by different methods and different fields – you can use one field, or more than one, as required.

Tasks that can be completed using database packages include:

- sorting data
- searching data
- the creation of mail merge letters when linked with word processing software.

# Spreadsheet

Spreadsheet packages enable a user to display and process data. They are capable of performing a wide range of calculations and so are generally used to process numerical data. However, a spreadsheet package can also handle text.

Tasks that can be completed using spreadsheet packages include:

- mathematical modelling
- modelling of objects
- producing graphs
- the use of 'what-if?' calculations
- goal seeking, forecasting (including trend lines) and data pattern analysis.

# Presentation

Presentation packages can be used to produce presentations to be shown to a target audience. They can be used for kiosk applications or presentations for speeches. They can run without intervention on a timer or with user intervention.

Tasks that can be completed using presentation packages include:

- presentations to be shown using printed acetate and an overhead projector
- presentations to be shown using a computer and digital projector.

# Web authoring

Web authoring, the creation of web pages, can be achieved by using a web authoring package or by using a word processing package and converting the document to a web page. Web authoring software has built-in functions to enable well designed web pages to be created with a variety of features to assist the needs of the user.

## Exam questions

1 Identify **two** tasks that could be carried out using word processing software. [*2 marks*]

2 Identify **two** tasks that could be carried out using spreadsheet software. [*2 marks*]

## Examiner hints and tips

Think about the following in relation to the questions opposite.

The questions ask for the identification of tasks carried out by different types of software packages. Your answers can include a word or phrase but they must be appropriate and relevant to the software given in the questions.

# Characteristics of applications

## Specification reference

**3.1.3b** – describe the characteristics of the following applications: school administration and teaching systems, stock control, booking systems, on-line training systems, timetabling and route finding systems, customer records systems and on-line banking systems.

## Keywords

**Just in time:** keeping stock that is held to a minimum through the use of ICT and logistics (transportation systems) so that materials are delivered on the day they are required.

**Booking system:** a system that enables users to book and pay for tickets, for example for travel or events.

**Data Protection Act (DPA):** an Act designed to regulate and safeguard data held by organisations about private individuals.

## Key points to remember

■ The common applications are used in business, commerce and education.

■ The characteristics of each application are specific to the task for which they are used.

| Application | Characteristics | Enable the user to |
|---|---|---|
| **School administration systems** | Used within schools and colleges to assist in the day-to-day running of the establishment. They can be related to pupils or staff. | ■ hold records <br> ■ record pupils' marks <br> ■ monitor attendance |
| **On-line banking** | Allow customers to access their bank account and carry out transactions using the internet. They are secure systems requiring logins and passwords. | ■ transfer money between accounts <br> ■ complete real-time transactions <br> ■ complete transactions remotely <br> ■ use BACS (bankers' automated clearing services) <br> ■ track payments into and out of accounts |
| **Stock control** | Stock control systems know how much of each item is in stock, when orders are due and how much stock is required on certain days. Some systems can order stock, updating records when stock is delivered. Stock control systems can be used for JIT (just in time) ordering. | ■ list all stock items and suppliers <br> ■ list all components for the item (if the stock is manufactured) <br> ■ know the minimum and maximum stock levels <br> ■ work out how much to order <br> ■ know the delivery times for stock items that have been ordered <br> ■ have links to the orders database |
| **Booking systems** | There are three main ways of booking – by telephone, by internet and by person/mail/fax. Booking systems require an event, a person and a date and time. | ■ select and check availability of an event, time and date <br> ■ specify, if applicable, the number of people <br> ■ check price of selected booking <br> ■ pay and confirm booking (via email or booking number) |

On-line banking

**In-car navigation system**

| Application | Characteristics | Enable the user to |
|---|---|---|
| **Route finders** | Route finding software allows the user to enter the starting and destination places and will plot a route between the two. This can be requested and printed from a website or through the use of in-car navigation systems. An in-car navigation system directs the user, confirming the location using GPS and adjusting its directions accordingly. | ■ specify where they are starting from and going to<br>■ specify the mode of travel – car, train or bus<br>■ specify places and roads you want to pass through or avoid<br>■ specify type of journey, for example, scenic, fastest or cheapest<br>■ save and print a route in a number of formats, for example, text and maps |
| **Customer records/ accounts** | Storing customer records and accounts is essential to the running of a business. The business must ensure they comply with the Data Protection Act (DPA). | ■ store contact details of customers<br>■ have a unique ID for each customer<br>■ store orders with a unique number<br>■ store orders against customers<br>■ generate invoices/credit notes for orders<br>■ store customer payments against the customer and invoice<br>■ produce customer statements and outstanding invoices<br>■ produce a list of products available<br>■ handle discounts and returns |
| **On-line training systems** | Enables people to study without a teacher. An on-line training system can be completed on the internet or by loading and running a storage media, such as a CD-ROM. | ■ follow a path of learning set by responses to previous questions<br>■ learn at their own pace<br>■ return to topics to reinforce concepts not fully understood<br>■ obtain feedback when tests are completed<br>■ use multimedia to enhance their learning experience<br>■ study at a time convenient to them |

## Exam question

**1** The organisers of a sports club use on-line banking to keep track of the club's income and expenditure.

Describe the characteristics of an on-line banking system.

[*6 marks*]

## Examiner hints and tips

Think about the following in relation to the above question.

The focus of the question is on the characteristics of an on-line banking system. Your answer should relate to these characteristics and how they can be used by the sports club.

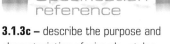 

# 3.3 Wizards, styles, templates and macros

## Specification reference

**3.1.3c –** describe the purpose and characteristics of wizards, styles, templates and macros, describing the advantages and disadvantages of their use.

###  Key points to remember

- Most standard/generic applications packages have features that can assist the user.

- Depending on the package, the use of the features may vary.

## Wizards

### Keywords

**Wizard:** assists the user in the production of the final product, for example a document, master slide or database.

**Style sheets:** used to set out the layout of documents. They can also be referred to as master documents.

**Macro:** a set of stored commands that can be replayed by pressing a combination of keys or by clicking a button.

A **wizard** presents options to the user that relate to the application. The user enters information into a range of screens. Once all the information has been entered the wizard is closed and the user is presented with the completed document containing the information in a pre-set format.

## Styles

Styles usually relate to word-processed documents or those produced using a desktop publishing (DTP) package and refer to complete documents. The use of a style ensures that all documents produced conform to a pre-determined layout, usually relating to the corporate image/house style. For example, this book has:

- Section headings, for example:

## Data and information

- Body text, for example:

   **Data** is a big part of our lives.

## Templates

A template provides standard pre-set layouts and formats, including the basic structure and settings of a document, such as page formatting, standard text and graphics. In presentation software templates specify the colour scheme as well as master slide and master title slide layouts. A document or presentation template can be created from scratch and saved to be used again.

# Macros

A **macro** enables the user to automate tasks that are performed on a regular basis. This is done by recording a series of commands to be run whenever that task needs to be performed. Macros can be used to give additional functionality to a spreadsheet, increasing the customisation of the interface. They can be activated through the use of a button placed on the toolbar, but will only run when the application program to which it is associated is being used. A macro will not run on its own or with a different application program.

| | Advantages | Disadvantages |
|---|---|---|
| Wizards | ■ They save time for the inexperienced user | ■ There is no individuality to the documents |
| | ■ They ensure that no important information is forgotten | ■ The documents may not fully meet the needs of the user |
| | ■ Standard formats can be used | ■ It can be difficult to tailor documents |
| | ■ There is an element of user friendliness | |
| Styles/templates | ■ A consistent house style is maintained | ■ The style needs to be developed before it can be used – this can take time and money |
| | ■ Different people can work on parts of documents which are consistent when collated | |
| Macros | ■ A repetitive task can be performed using a simple instruction (e.g. key press or button click) | ■ Error messages may occur if the conditions when the macro is run are different from those when it was recorded |
| | ■ Errors may be reduced, as the instructions included in the macro are run automatically and are the same every time | ■ To correct any errors the user must have some knowledge of how the macro was recorded |
| | ■ Inexperienced users can perform complex tasks by using a pre-recorded macro | ■ If the macro is run from a different starting point from that intended then it may go wrong |
| | | ■ Users must know and remember the key combinations to run the macro |
| | | ■ As a macro is pre-programmed it may not do what the user wants |

## Exam question

**1** Describe **two** advantages and **one** disadvantage of using a wizard to create a presentation. [6 marks]

### Examiner hints and tips

Think about the following in relation to the above question.

The focus of the question is on wizards and presentation software. The answer you give must only relate to presentation software. You have been asked to provide two advantages and only one disadvantage.

# 3.4 Tailored data-entry screens

**Specification reference**

**3.1.3d** – describe the design considerations for tailored data-entry screens.

## Key points to remember

- Data-entry screens can be tailored in either a database or a spreadsheet package.

- The screen should be tailored to meet the needs and expertise of the user.

### Keyword

**Form:** a type of user interface where the user types in data in spaces provided on the screen.

### Weblink

**http://cisnet.baruch.cuny.edu/ holowczak/classes/2200/access/ access7.html**

Hints and tips related to data-entry forms.

## Generic design considerations

- Use the house style or corporate image to ensure a consistent layout.

- Colours should be easy to read and not clash.

- The font style and size used for text should be clear and easy to read.

- Graphics and animations should be fit for purpose and kept to a minimum.

- Messages should be useful, clear and provide help and assistance in simple and natural language.

- The on-screen information should be in a logical order and flow down the screen.

- The interface should be easy to learn and use.

- Exits should be clearly marked.

- Commonly used functions should be given a short-cut/button/ menu option.

## Forms

The interface of a database package is, usually, not very user friendly. The average user would struggle to complete their required tasks unless the interface was tailored.

The interface for a database is likely to be through the use of **forms**. Forms can be created in one of three ways:

- within the application

- using web-based forms

- using third party programs, such as a programming language, to access and manipulate the data.

# Additional design considerations for forms

**Consistency** – buttons and data-entry boxes should be in the same place on all forms. The format of text to enter should always be the same. Text style and colours used should also be the same. If data is taken from a paper form then the on-screen form should be consistent.

**Relevance** – no redundant material should be asked for. The information requested should require the minimum of input and user actions. The user should carry out the minimum of keystrokes to complete a task.

**Supportiveness** – the form should not give too much or too little information to the user. Just enough information should be given to support the user when completing the task.

**Visual and audible cues** – these are used to give feedback to the user to confirm actions or notify them of an error. Visual cues include the use of the colour red to denote an error. A 'happy' sound could denote a correct keystroke or entry. Error messages should be helpful.

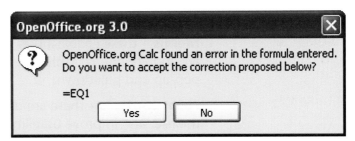

Error message

**Intuitiveness** – each time the system is used the user must be able to remember what to do. The interface/form must be appropriate for completing the task and reflect the user's knowledge and understanding.

## Exam question

**1** Describe **two** considerations that should be taken into account when designing a data-entry form.                    [*4 marks*]

## Examiner hints and tips

Think about the following in relation to the above question.

> The question refers to a data-entry form. You can focus on the generic considerations for designing a user interface or focus on the specific design considerations for a form. The answer you give must relate to the design considerations and not to how the user will use the form. You will need to identify the design consideration and then go on to provide further description.

# 3.5 Tailoring standard/generic applications software 1

## Specification reference

**3.1.3e** – describe how standard/generic applications software can be tailored using buttons, forms, form controls, menus and templates and give examples of the use of each.

## Keywords

**Form:** a type of user interface where the user types in data in spaces provided on the screen.

**Menu:** a list of options from which the user can select.

## Key point to remember

■ An interface can be tailored to meet the user's needs through the use of buttons, forms, menus and form controls.

**Buttons** – these can be pushed by the user to start an event. They can be used to link to a macro or to run a selected action/command. For example, a command button can be added to a user interface to run a search, or to sort or edit data. A button can also display pictures or text.

**Forms** – these can be used to assist in the entry of data and to give help and guidance on what data should be input. They can include instructions to the user, validation and error messages. Forms may include drop down boxes, option boxes and fill-in boxes.

**Menus** – these enable a user to select actions, showing those that are and are not available. There are three main types – full-screen, pop-up and pull-down.

**Form controls** – these are used to increase the interactivity with the user and improve usability. Some examples of form controls are:

 Option button – options can be selected and given values.

 Check box – options can be ticked.

 Combo box – items can be selected from a drop down box.

## Exam question

**1** Describe, using examples, how form controls can be used to customise a user interface. [6 marks]

## Examiner hints and tips

Think about the following in relation to the above question.

The question refers to the customisation of a user interface with the focus on form controls. The question also asks you to provide examples. It is unlikely that, if you forget to provide examples, you will achieve all the marks allocated. You should aim to provide at least three examples of form controls as well as describing how they can be used.

**3.6** # Tailoring standard/generic applications software 2

**Specification reference**

**3.1.3f** – explain the advantages and disadvantages of tailoring standard/generic applications software.

 **Key point to remember**

■ There are advantages and disadvantages to tailoring standard/generic applications software.

 **Keyword**

**Standard/generic applications software:** software that is provided for a range of tasks rather than one specific task, for example word processing or spreadsheet software.

## Advantages

■ The simplification of user data entry, leading to fewer mistakes by the user.

■ Forms, buttons, menus and macros can be used to reduce the time taken to enter data.

■ Data entered can be validated on entry.

■ The interface is simplified, which assists novice users.

## Disadvantages

■ A high level of technical knowledge is required to create and test the interface.

■ If changes need to be made to the user interface then this can take time.

■ If the software used to build the interface is upgraded, then the interface may not work as needed or intended.

■ If a problem occurs with any component of the interface, then the user may not be able to complete the tasks.

## Exam question

**1** Explain the advantages of tailoring a spreadsheet to provide a user interface. [6 marks]

### Examiner hints and tips

Think about the following in relation to the above question.

The question refers to tailoring a spreadsheet to provide a user interface. You should consider the tasks the users are most likely to carry out using a spreadsheet and then explain the advantages of creating a user interface. Examples will enhance your answer to the question, but remember that the focus is on the use of a spreadsheet.

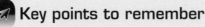

## 3.7 House style 1

**Specification reference**

**3.1.3g** – explain why an organisation needs a consistent house style.

**Keywords**

**House style:** a set of rules that must be followed for all documents sent out by an organisation so that they maintain a consistent appearance. This helps the public to become familiar with an organisation's 'look'.

**Weblink**

**http://docs.paperless-school.com/ HouseStyle**

A discussion about house styles.

### Key points to remember

- A consistent house style makes the business easily recognisable.
- Logos are part of a company's or organisation's house style.

The logos below are immediately recognisable and help the public to relate to a company or organisation.

**Familiar logos**

A **house style** will define the fonts, paragraph styles and graphics that can be used, as well as the layout of documents.

Through the use of a house style it is less likely that important information will be missed off documents as templates and macros are used to design standard documents.

A design team is used to develop a consistent house style. If the house style is not used then this process is a waste of time and money.

A house style enables different people to work on parts of the same document and use the same style and templates. This allows the integration of several documents from different teams into a final document or presentation.

### Exam question

**1** Explain why it is important for a company to have a consistent house style. [4 marks]

### Examiner hints and tips

Think about the following in relation to the above question.

The question refers to a company having a consistent house style. You will need to consider the different documents produced by the company. The answer you give must also consider the production of the documents, how they are used and the impact they will have on the public and the company.

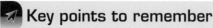

## 3.8 | House style 2

**Specification reference**

**3.1.3h –** describe how master documents/slides, style sheets and templates can be used to create a consistent house style.

### Key points to remember

- A consistent house style can be maintained through the use of master documents/slides, style sheets and templates.
- A house style can be maintained whilst different people work on different parts of a document or presentation.

### Keywords

**Master document/slide:** used to set the features that will appear on every page or slide, including background and text colours, position of frames and the font styles and sizes.

**Style sheets:** used to set out the layout of documents.

**Master slide** – this shows the theme, the position of any graphics (for example, the company logo) and the position of information which must appear on each slide, such as the date, slide number and any footer/header text. It defines master text (font type, size and colour), as well as background colour and any special effects. Master slides are developed to maintain the company house style on all presentations.

**Master document** – this is a collection or set of separate files that can be used to manage a multipart document. The master document template controls the styles used to ensure they conform to the house style.

**Style sheets** – these are also referred to as master documents. They are very similar to paragraph styles but refer to complete documents. Using them ensures that all documents produced conform to the house style but still gives scope for creativity.

**Templates** – in word-processing, these are standard documents that determine and define the house style layout/structure and format of different documents. They include page and text formatting, standard text and graphics. In presentation software, a design template specifies the colour scheme as well as master slide and master title slide layouts with custom formatting and fonts.

### Exam question

**1** Describe how a master slide can ensure that a presentation follows the company house style. [4 marks]

### Examiner hints and tips

Think about the following in relation to the above question.

The question refers to a presentation following the house style. The focus of your answer must be on presentations and how master slides can be used.

## 3.9 | Importing and exporting files

### Specification reference

**3.1.3i** – describe how to import/ export files between standard/generic applications with no common format.

### Keywords

**File type:** files can have many different types, depending on the type of data they contain and the software used to create them. The file type is given as a three letter extension to the filename, separated by a full stop, for example .doc, .bmp.

**txt and rtf (rich text format):** file types used for converting text files.

**CSV (comma separated variable) and TSV (tab separated variable):** file types used for converting spreadsheets or tables of data.

**DBF (database file) and CSV:** file types used for converting databases.

### 🚀 Key points to remember

- Different file types are suited to different applications.
- All software vendors create their own methods of storing files, with different applications also storing the files in different formats.

When the operating system is installed different **file types** are allocated to programs. This means the operating system knows which program to start when a user wishes to open a file.

Knowing the file extension or the type of file can help the user when searching for files. Sometimes data stored in one application needs to be used in another. The data will need to be converted. There are two standard procedures for converting files from one format to another.

## Option 1

Package A can save the file in Package B's format.

### Procedure

- Open the file in Package A (Open).
- Save as or export to the Package B format (Convert).
- Open in Package B and save (Save).

## Option 2

Package A cannot save to Package C's format.

### Procedure

- Open the file in Package A (Open).
- Save as or export to a format common to Package A and Package B (Convert).
- Open the file in Package B (Import).
- Convert to the format required by Package C (Convert).
- Save in the new format (Save).

### Exam question

**1** A file needs to be transferred from a spreadsheet to a database.

Describe the process that would need to be completed.

[*4 marks*]

### Examiner hints and tips

Think about the following in relation to the question opposite.

> You must ensure that the process is given in the correct order. The question relates to transferring a file from a spreadsheet to a database. Your answer should include step 1 as being 'Open file in spreadsheet' and the final step as 'Open file in database'.

## 3.10 Users' needs

### Specification reference

**3.1.3j** – explain the needs of different users of standard/generic applications software.

### 🔑 Keyword

**Thesaurus:** a program that offers alternative words with a similar meaning.

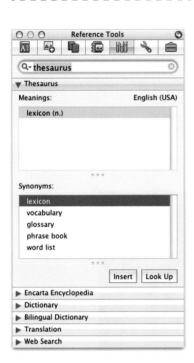

### ⚡ Key point to remember

■ Different users need different things from the software they use.

Different users need different things from the software they use. For example, a secretary, a translator and a technical author will have very different requirements for a word processor:

**Secretary** – needs a wide range of fonts, spelling and grammar checking facilities and templates. Functions that are used the most will need to be readily available, for example mail merge, templates and saving/back-up.

**Translator** – needs to convert a document from one language to another. They will need the software to have a language specific dictionary and the ability to insert language specific characters.

**Scientific author** – needs the software to be able to carry out automatic section numbering, indexing and formatting into a report style. They will also need a specialist technical dictionary and **thesaurus**.

### Exam question

**1** Describe the software features that enable a secretary to send mail merge letters to the customers of a company.      [4 marks]

### Examiner hints and tips

Think about the following in relation to the above question.

The question refers to a secretary and a very specific task that has to be carried out. The answer you give must be applied to this scenario. The question does not mention the software that will be used, so you should focus on giving the features that will be used during mail merge.

# 4 Spreadsheet concepts

## 4.1 Modelling software

**Specification reference**

**3.1.4a** – describe the characteristics of modelling software and give reasons why a model might be used.

### Keywords

**Spreadsheet software:** An application consisting of a table of rows and columns. Cells can contain labels, data or formulae that enable automatic calculations to be carried out.

**Variables:** values entered into a cell to be used in a formula. They can be changed which leads to recalculation of the figures.

**Constants:** values which are used in formulae but that cannot be changed.

### Weblink

http://www.bbc.co.uk/
schools/gcsebitesize/ict/
modelling/0spreadsheetsrev1.shtml

BBC site offering basic concepts of spreadsheets.

### Key point to remember

- There are two main types of modelling used in ICT:
  - ▶ Modelling of objects (rooms, buildings, cars, etc.)
  - ▶ Mathematical modelling (financial, calculations, spreadsheets, etc.)

### Modelling of objects

Computer models allow you to create a natural representation of an object:

**A computer model of a building**

- The effect of external influences (for example, earthquakes, fire and explosions) can also be modelled.

- Different attributes of the building can be shown. For example, external views, electrical wiring circuits or the building frame.

- The model can be rotated and parts shown in more detail by zooming in on them.

Questions can be asked of the model. For example, changing the components to see how different materials look or react, moving items or changing the layout and design.

### Mathematical modelling

Models which represent mathematical elements are usually done using **spreadsheet software**. These are based on rows and columns so sequencing can be used.

Functions and formulae allow numbers to be input and for any changes to be automatically recalculated. Many different scenarios can be tried out using a single model.

'What-if?' questions allow values to be changed to see the effect.

An alternative method of asking questions is to start with the goal and to model alternative ways of reaching the same result – this is known as goal seeking.

| | A | B | C | D | E | F | G |
|---|---|---|---|---|---|---|---|
| 1 | | | Sales by Groups of Item Each Quarter | | | | |
| 2 | | | | | | | |
| 3 | | 1st quarter | 2nd quarter | 3rd quarter | 4th quarter | Total sales | |
| 4 | Pens | 576 | 454 | 876 | 343 | 2249 | |
| 5 | Pencils | 345 | 232 | 545 | 323 | 1445 | |
| 6 | Pads of paper | 54 | 45 | 76 | 43 | 218 | |
| 7 | | | | | | | |
| 8 | Total sales | 975 | 731 | 1497 | 709 | 3912 | |
| 9 | | | | | | | |
| 10 | | | | | | | |
| 11 | | | | | | | |
| 12 | | | | | | | |
| 13 | | | | | | | |

**A mathematical model**

- **Variables** and **constants** can be used.

- Individual cells or ranges of cells can be given names. This makes formulae easier to understand.

- Multiple worksheets and graphical representation of data can be used.

- Absolute and relative cell referencing can be used.

## ■ Why is modelling used?

This is covered in section 4.6 – Spreadsheet simulations.

### Exam questions

**1** Explain the characteristics of software used to model objects.

[6 marks]

**2** Describe how functions and formulae can be used in mathematical modelling. [4 marks]

### Examiner hints and tips

Think about the following in relation to the above questions.

**Question 1:** The question relates to the use of software used for modelling objects. The answer you give must focus on this; you must not relate your answer to the use of software to model mathematical scenarios.

**Question 2:** The question focus is on two specific characteristics with 2 marks allocated to each characteristic. You will also need to relate your answer to mathematical modelling.

# 4.2 Variables, formulae, rules and functions

## Specification reference

**3.1.4b** – explain how variables, formulae, rules and functions are used in modelling software.

## 🔑 Keywords

**Variable:** a name associated with a particular memory location used to store data. Variables are used because they allow data to be stored, retrieved and manipulated without knowing in advance what the data will be.

**Formula:** a mathematical expression entered into a spreadsheet cell, whose value is automatically calculated and entered into the cell, for example 4*A3 or E5+F5.

## 🚀 Key points to remember

- A model has four main characteristics that allow it to manipulate numbers and text.
- A model has features that will enable:
  - ▶ Recalculation of values when a number changes.
  - ▶ Questions to be asked and answered with the minimum amount of effort.
  - ▶ Different scenarios to be tested.

### ■ Variables

A **variable** is an identifier associated with a particular cell that contains a value. A variable could be a cell reference (e.g. A3), or a cell name (e.g. VAT_RATE). When a variable is used in a spreadsheet, it is the value contained within the variable that is used.

### ■ Formulae

A **formula** is the way that a calculation is represented in a spreadsheet. Formulae use numbers, addresses of cell references or names and mathematical operators (such as + / * −). An example of a formula is:

$$B6+(B6*VAT\_RATE)$$

### ■ Rules

Rules are a set of procedures that must be followed. A rule can also be the sequence of events required for the calculation to work. Rules enable a procedure to be followed by different people and a comparable result obtained. A validation rule can be applied to make sure that the value is given.

### ■ Functions

Functions are predefined, complex formulae. They represent standard routines used to perform common tasks. They use reserved words that are built into the spreadsheet, for example MAX, MIN and SUM.

## Exam question

**1** Describe **two** differences between a formula and a function.
[*4 marks*]

## Examiner hints and tips

Think about the following in relation to the question opposite.

The question refers to the differences between a formula and a function. You must provide clear descriptions of the differences between each. A simple response that ends 'and the other does not' is unlikely to get many, if any, marks.

**'What-if?' questions**

## Specification reference

**3.1.4c –** describe how a data model may be used for answering 'what-if?' questions and explain the advantages of being able to answer such questions using a spreadsheet.

### Keywords

**Modelling:** creating a computer model of a real-world situation so that variables can be changed to answer 'what-if?' questions.

**What-if?:** the use of spreadsheets and modelling enables the user to change specific values, so that results are recalculated, to answer questions that start 'what-if?'

### Key points to remember

■ A 'what-if?' question is used to predict the future.

■ A value is changed and other values are then recalculated.

## ■ Data models

Models contain features which can help to answer '**what-if?**' questions. These include:

■ Calculations

■ Formulae

■ Functions

■ Rules

■ Cell references

■ Named cells.

## Benefits

■ Models can automatically recalculate data. The model can be changed many times and lots of different values and figures looked at. The only cost involved is time.

■ When the model has been created it can be used to answer unlimited 'what-if?' questions.

■ Models can present data as text, numbers or graphs.

■ Models can have interfaces built to increase usability.

■ The cost and time are both likely to be less than creating physical models.

■ Virtual models of buildings can be tested using many different scenarios without being destroyed.

■ If an error is found it is simpler and faster to alter it on a computer than in a physical model. A rule or function may need rewriting which can be done quickly.

## Exam question

**1** Explain **two** advantages of using a spreadsheet to answer 'what-if?' questions.

[*4 marks*]

### Examiner hints and tips

Think about the following in relation to the question opposite.

The question refers to the use of a spreadsheet to answer 'what-if?' questions. You must focus your answer on the use of a spreadsheet and not, for example, CAD.

# Components of spreadsheet software

## Specification reference

**3.1.4d** – describe and explain the purpose and use of worksheets, workbooks, rows, columns, cells and ranges in spreadsheet software.

## Keywords

**Worksheet:** a single sheet of rows and columns in a spreadsheet package.

**Workbook:** a set of linked worksheets in a spreadsheet package.

**Rows:** a horizontal group of cells in a spreadsheet. They are normally identified with numbers.

**Columns:** a vertical group of cells in a spreadsheet.

### Key points to remember

■ A spreadsheet is made up of different parts.
■ Each part has a different function and purpose.

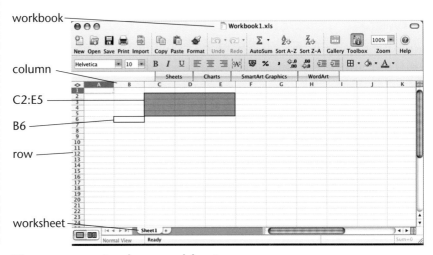

**The components of a spreadsheet**

## ■ The components of a spreadsheet

**Worksheet** – also known as a sheet or spreadsheet in some applications. A worksheet is a large grid of cells on a single sheet and can be given a name. It can be used to hold data on a single area of a business, for example sales data, expenditure or stock.

**Workbook** – a collection of worksheets. If each worksheet contains a separate area of the business, workbooks contain data about the entire business. If data is changed on one worksheet, this will be reflected across the whole workbook. You can assign different access rights to different worksheets. A workbook is saved as a single entity so it is easy to back up, copy and send to other people. All the data required is in a single location.

**Rows and columns** – these are used to organise the data. They can hold headings and/or the data. The width and height can be altered to make sure all the contents are clearly visible. They can also be hidden from the user.

**Cell** – this is an individual data store identified by a unique row and column identifier. In the example above, the highlighted cell is in Column B and Row 6, that is **B6**. Names can also be used as unique identifiers. Each cell can be formatted and protected independently.

**Ranges** – a group of cells that can be given a name or identified by their cell references. In the example above the range reference is **C2:E5**. The cells within a range usually contain similar data. They are often used in formulae and functions and the same formatting may be applied to all of the cells in a range.

## Exam questions

A car hire company keeps records on a spreadsheet.

**1** Explain how the car hire company could use a range in the spreadsheet. *[4 marks]*

**2** Explain how the car hire company could make use of workbooks. *[4 marks]*

**3** Describe **two** advantages to the car hire company of giving a cell a name instead of using the column and row identifier. *[4 marks]*

### Examiner hints and tips

Think about the following in relation to the above questions. The three questions refer to a car hire company. They must all be answered within the context of this company.

**Questions 1 and 2:** The questions relate to the use of specific features – ranges and workbooks. You need to refer the use of these features to the car hire company. As with other questions where there is a context, generic answers will not be awarded full marks.

**Question 3:** The focus of the question is on the advantages of giving a cell a name, with 2 marks allocated to each advantage. You need to provide answers in the context of the car hire company to get full marks.

## 4.5 | Cell referencing

**Specification reference**

**3.1.4e** – describe absolute and relative cell referencing, and give examples of uses of each method.

### 🔑 Keywords

**Absolute referencing:** when the cell referenced in a spreadsheet formula remains exactly the same when the formula is copied to other cells.

**Relative referencing:** when the cell referenced in a spreadsheet formula changes when the formula is copied to other cells.

### ⤴ Key points to remember

■ Cell referencing is the use of cell identifiers to include the value contained within the cell in a formula or function.

■ There are two ways the cell reference can be affected – absolute and relative.

## ■ Absolute referencing

- Used when a cell referenced in a formula needs to remain exactly the same when the formula is copied to other cells.

- The referenced cell usually contains a constant value.

- The cell is denoted by the use of the $ sign, for example $A$1, or by naming the cell, for example VAT_RATE.

Benefits include if the value that has been referenced needs to change then only one cell needs to be changed. The value in the cell can be used in many functions and formulae.

## ■ Relative referencing

- Used when a cell referenced in a formula changes when the formula is copied to other cells.

- The cell referenced is relative to the cell that contains the formula. For example, if the formula A3+A4 is copied into an adjoining cell on the right then it becomes B3+B4.

- Column references are changed by the same amount so that the correct cell reference is shown.

- Used when the user wants the cell reference to change when they copy a cell.

Benefits include ensuring that the correct cells are referenced when cells are copied to new rows.

### Exam question

**1** Describe, using examples relating to a car repair garage, the difference between absolute and relative cell referencing.

[*6 marks*]

### Examiner hints and tips

Think about the following in relation to the question opposite.

The question refers to the differences between absolute and relative cell referencing. You must provide descriptions of the differences between each. The examples you use in your answer must relate to a car repair garage and not be generic.

## 4.6 Spreadsheet simulations

### Specification reference

**3.1.4f** – explain the advantages and disadvantages of using a spreadsheet to create and run simulations.

### Keyword

**Modelling:** creating a computer model of a real-world situation so that variables can be changed to answer 'what-if?' questions.

### Weblink

**www.funderstanding.com/K12/coaster**

Fun simulation for building a rollercoaster.

### Key points to remember

- A spreadsheet is usually used to create and run financial models but all modelling (financial and objects) is based on mathematics.
- A model consists of a set of data and a set of rules that control what the data does.

A spreadsheet, when used for **modelling**, has many advantages and disadvantages:

## Advantages

- 'What-if?' questions can be asked.
- Automatic recalculation.
- Graphs can be produced.
- Variables and constants can be used.
- The model can be saved centrally or shared between different people in different locations.
- It can be quicker and cheaper to build a computer-based model. Only one model needs to be built which can then be changed.
- It can be safer to run a simulation/model under extreme conditions than to build an actual model and test it.
- Computer-based models can be speeded up or slowed down to see effects that are difficult to see in real time.

## Disadvantages

- The model may not be an accurate representation of the real world, especially if people are involved.
- Many variables may need to be considered and it is easy to miss things out.
- Producing an effective model may be time-consuming and running the model may need expensive hardware and software.

### Exam question

1 Explain **two** advantages of using a spreadsheet to model the financial accounts of a shop. [4 marks]

### Examiner hints and tips

Think about the following in relation to the question opposite.

The question focuses on the use of a spreadsheet to model financial accounts, so your answer must relate to financial modelling. The examples you use must relate to a shop and not be generic.

## 5.1  Database terms

### Specification reference

**3.1.5a** – describe the terms typically used in relational database terminology: tables, primary keys, fields, records, relationships, foreign keys, duplicate data, referential integrity, entity, attribute, explaining the role and purpose of each.

### Key points to remember

- Databases have a lot of related terminology.
- A table is made up of records.
- Records are made up of fields.
- Fields are made up of characters.

| | CustomerID | Forename | Surname | Address 1 | Town | County |
|---|---|---|---|---|---|---|
| | 1 | Jim | Carroll | 2 The Grange | Spittal | Dyfed |
| | 2 | Mary | Handy | 4 The High Street | Splatt | Devon |
| | 3 | Sue | Weeks | 1 The End | Boot | Cumbria |
| | 4 | James | Jordan | 45 Road Close | Eden | Cumbria |

Field · Names · Records · Table · Primary key · Data items

**Database terminology**

### Keyword

**Relationships:** the links between tables in a relational database. They include:

- One-to-many
- Many-to-many
- One-to-one

### Weblink

**http://www.geekgirls.com/ database_dictionary.htm**

Definitions and summary of database terms.

## Table

A table contains data about 'things' and is made up of records. It can also be known as a relation. A table is a data structure made up of rows and columns that contains data about the items and must have a unique name.

## Record

A record is a single row within a table. It is a collection of data about a single item or a single event. They are made up of fields and can contain different data types. In a table, each record must be unique.

## Field

A field is an individual data item within a record. Each field within a record should have a unique name and only contain a single data item. Fields have individual data types and can have their own validation.

## Primary key

The most important key. This is a field, in the table, that allows each record to be uniquely identified. Every value of the primary key must be unique.

## Foreign key

A foreign key is used to link tables together. A foreign key is a field in one table that is linked to a primary key in another table. The data types of the fields that are linked must be the same.

## Relationships

There are three types of **relationship** that can be identified as existing between entities:

- One-to-one
- One-to-many
- Many-to-many

(More detail is given in section 5.2 – Relationships.)

## Entity

An entity is the name given to anything you can store data about, for example CUSTOMER, SUPPLIER or ORDER. They are referred to singularly and always written in capitals. Entity names should be single words.

## Attribute

An attribute is a characteristic of an entity. For example, one of the attributes of the entity CUSTOMER would be 'surname'.

## Duplicate data

Duplicate data is data that exists in two tables. Duplicate data is removed from a database through the process of normalisation and the linking of tables through relationships.

## Referential integrity

Referential integrity makes sure that it is impossible to enter a reference in a database to a link which does not exist.

## Exam question

**1** A database contains tables, records and fields. Using examples from a school, describe the terms tables, records and fields.

[*6 marks*]

## Examiner hints and tips

Think about the following in relation to the question opposite.

The question asks for a description of three database terms. But it also requires you to provide examples related to a school. The examples you give must be appropriate to a school and relate to the term you are describing.

If you provide examples not related to a school then you are unlikely to gain full marks for the question.

5.2 # Relationships

## Specification reference

**3.1.5b** – identify tables, records, fields, primary keys and foreign keys, and define relationships between entities using an entity relationship diagram (ERD) for a given scenario.

### Keyword

**Entity relationship diagram (ERD):** a diagram that shows the relationships between entities in a database. At this level, entities can be thought of as tables. Relationships (one-to-one, one-to-many and many-to-many) are also referred to as the degree of the relationship.

### Weblink

**http://www.getahead-direct.com/gw-er-diagram-tutorial.htm**

Tutorial on drawing an entity relationship diagram.

## Key points to remember

- The relationship definitions were learnt in the previous section – this section is about using and implementing those definitions.
- When drawing a relationship, remember that the many end usually links to a foreign key.

## Identifying entities

For any given scenario, you will need to identify the tables required. For example:

A company stores information on products, customers, suppliers and orders.

You will need to identify the tables that would be needed to store this information. Having identified the tables, you need to identify fields for that table – remember to include the primary key and, if necessary, the foreign key:

SUPPLIER: SupplierID, Name, Address Line 1, Address Line 2, Town, County, Postcode, Email, Telephone, Contact.

## Types of relationship

There are three relationships that can be identified as existing between entities:

**One-to-one:** One record in one table can only be linked to one record in another table.

**One-to-many:** One record in one table can be linked to many records in another table.

**Many-to-many:** Many records in one table can be linked to many records in another table (these need resolving into 1:1/1:M).

You may be asked to identify the degree of the relationship between entities (think of entities as another word for tables).

### Examiner hints and tips

Think about the following in relation to the questions opposite.

**Question 1:** There are 4 marks here but only three obvious tables. There is a second book table that needs considering.

**Question 2:** The tables are given and you need to decide on the degree of the relationship and draw an ERD.

## Exam questions

1 Identify the entities required for a library system involving books, customers and loans. [4 marks]

2 Draw an ERD for a pogo stick retailer that has the following tables: Supplier, Product, Order, Order Details, Customer. [4 marks]

## 5.3 Different normal forms

### Specification reference

**3.1.5c** – identify the characteristics of data in unnormalised form (0NF), first normal form (1NF), second normal form (2NF) and third normal form (3NF).

### Keyword

**Atomic:** the data value cannot be broken down any further.

### Weblink

**http://databases.about.com/od/ specificproducts/a/normalization. htm**

Help, advice and guidance on normalisation.

### Key points to remember

- The process of normalisation reduces data redundancy and inconsistency, and makes it easier to use and maintain data.
- There are specific rules attached to each normal form.

## Unnormalised form (0NF)

When data is first collected and put into a table, it is in unnormalised form – UNF or 0NF.

## First normal form (1NF)

This is the first stage of normalising a data model and involves ensuring that all data items are **atomic** and that there are no repeating fields. To be in first normal form (1NF):

- Each table must have a primary key.
- Each field name is unique.
- There are no repeating fields in a single record.
- All data within a field is atomic.

## Second normal form (2NF)

This is the second stage of normalising a data model. A table is in second normal form (2NF) if all its non-key attributes are dependent on the entire primary key. To be in 2NF:

- The table must already be in 1NF.
- All of the non-key fields can be found by using the entire primary key.

## Third normal form (3NF)

This is the third stage of normalising a data model. The third normal form (3NF) involves ensuring that every attribute of an entity that is not part of the primary key is wholly dependent on that key. To be in 3NF:

- The table must already be in 2NF.
- All non-key items must be fully dependent on the primary key.

### Exam question

**1** Identify the characteristics of data in 2NF and 3NF.
[*4 marks*]

### Examiner hints and tips

Think about the following in relation to the question opposite.

The focus of this question is on the characteristics of data in 2NF and 3NF. You do not need to describe the process of data moving from 2NF to 3NF.

## 5.4 Normalisation

### Specification reference

**3.1.5d** – describe the advantages and disadvantages of normalisation.

### Keyword

**Normalisation:** the process of refining a data model.

### Weblink

**http://www.datamodel.org/ NormalizationRules.html**

Information about normalisation.

### Key points to remember

■ Normalisation gives many advantages to the database that emerges at the end of the process.

■ There are also disadvantages to normalising a database.

## Advantages of normalisation

- Removes redundant and duplicate data. This saves on storage space.

- Easier maintenance – as the data is not duplicated an update on a single piece of data will mean that any process that uses the data can be relied upon.

- Increases data consistency.

- Increases integrity.

- Provides flexibility if expansion is required. If the requirements of the organisation using the data change, the database can be adapted without a major redesign of the structure.

## Disadvantages of normalisation

- Reduced database performance. A normalised database requires greater use of the CPU, memory and input/output.

- Normalisation is not appropriate for some types of database. For example, unnormalised data is better for reporting systems (because it is likely that the data is in a structure suitable for the reports) and databases that store historical data.

### Exam question

**1** Describe the advantages of normalisation. [4 marks]

### Examiner hints and tips

Think about the following in relation to the above question.

The question asks for the advantages of normalisation. You should identify the advantages and expand on each of them.

## 5.5 Data dictionary

### Specification reference

**3.1.5e** – describe the components of a data dictionary.

### Keyword

**Data dictionary:** contains details of all the entities and attributes in a system. This will include the name of each, as well as the data type, format or length and any validation required.

### Weblink

**http://www.ss64.com/orad/index. html**

An example of a data dictionary.

### Key points to remember

- The data dictionary is often called 'a database about a database'.
- A data dictionary contains metadata (data about data).

Different database packages will contain slightly different information in the data dictionary. The table below shows the basic data that would be expected in them all.

| Data | Description |
| --- | --- |
| Table Name | The name of the table. A unique name for each table in the database |
| Field Name | Each field is identified |
| Field Data Type | The data type allocated to each field: text/string/date/Boolean, etc. |
| Field Length | The number of characters allocated for the contents of the field |
| Field Default Value | If a field has a default value that automatically appears on the creation of a new record |
| Field Validation | Any validation applied to the field |
| Table Security | Who has access to write, update, edit, delete, etc. values to and from the table |
| Keys | Primary and foreign keys are identified |
| Indexes | Any field which is indexed |
| Relationships | Relationships between tables identified: one-to-one, etc. |

### Exam question

**1** Describe the components of a data dictionary that relate to tables. [*4 marks*]

### Examiner hints and tips

Think about the following in relation to the above question.

The focus of this question is on a data dictionary and the components that relate to tables. If you answer with components that are not related to tables, for example fields, then you are unlikely to gain many marks.

**5.6** **Data types**

### Specification reference

**3.1.5f** – select appropriate data types for a given set of data, and explain the advantages and disadvantages of alternative data types.

### Keyword

**Data types:** the type of data that can be held in a location such as a field in a database. Examples include integer and Boolean.

### Key points to remember

- There are five main data types.
- The data type selected should be appropriate to the data being held.

## Data types

The main **data types** available are:

- Text/string
- Integer
- Real
- Boolean
- Date/time.

### Text/string

Text/string is the use of any key on the keyboard. It can be used to store text (Mr Brown), text and numbers (CQ5 9EB), or just numbers (42).

Numbers are only stored as text if no calculations are to be performed on them, for example telephone numbers.

### Integer

Integers are numbers without a decimal place, for example 3 and 97.

### Real

Real numbers are those with a decimal place, for example 42.9 and 7.2. Currency is usually stored as a real number, for example £76.00 (the £ symbol, although text, is stored separately).

### Boolean

Boolean fields can store one of only two possible values, for example yes/no and true/false.

They are used to represent any question with two possible outcomes, for example male/female or video/DVD.

### Date/time

This data type is used for defining dates and time. It can be set so that each time the date and time are accessed they will show the current date and time. Date/time data types can also be used to calculate the difference between the start date/time and end date/time.

## Advantages and disadvantages

The advantages and disadvantages of using the different data types are related to their use within a given scenario and what the data will be used for.

For example, if the data for a field – 'Does the house have a garage?' – has only two possible options – Yes or No. This is appropriate for a Boolean data type, because it takes up the minimal amount of memory space and can be validated to ensure the data stored is one of those two values. It also enables easier searching of the data.

### Exam question

**1** Data about customers is stored in a database. Identify the data type that should be used for each field given in the table below. *[4 marks]*

| Field | Data type |
| --- | --- |
| Surname | |
| Postcode | |
| Telephone number | |
| Loyalty scheme member | |

### Examiner hints and tips

Think about the following in relation to the above question.

The table must be completed to show one data type for each field. If you provide more than one data type for each field only the first one will be marked.

You must select the most appropriate data type. It may help to think about an example of each field before you write your answer in the data type column.

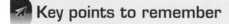

## 5.7 Queries

### Specification reference

**3.1.5g** – describe dynamic and static parameter queries and simple and complex queries and explain when and how they might be used.

### Keyword

**Parameter:** the value used by a query to select records.

### Weblink

**http://www.fontstuff.com/access/ acctut01.htm**

Website related to parameter queries.

### Key points to remember

- Databases can run queries to search for specific records.
- Queries can be static or dynamic, simple or complex.

## ■ Parameter queries

Parameter queries return fields from tables where the value of the **parameter** is matched. They can be static, dynamic, simple or complex:

- **Static parameter queries** – these cannot be changed. They are 'hardcoded'. This means that every time the query is run the same parameters will be searched for.

- **Dynamic parameter queries** – these can be created to ask the user for the value to search for.

  For example, a dialogue box, like the one shown below, can be created. This takes a value from the user and uses it in the query.

In general, dynamic queries are more useful than static queries.

- **Simple parameter queries** – these have only one parameter value. The dialogue box in the example above shows a simple search on one field, namely Supplier.

- **Complex parameter queries** – these search using more than one parameter value, that is using two or more criteria. A complex query can contain as many parameters as are needed.

The dialogue box below shows a complex search for 'Jones The Penmaker' with a contact name of 'Smith'.

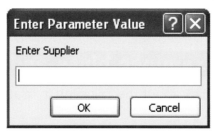

The parameters can be joined using:

- AND
- OR
- NOT

**AND** – will include all records found from both parameter queries.

**OR** – will find records that match one or the other or both parameter searches.

**NOT** – an inverse query.

Parameter queries do not have to match values exactly; they can make use of:

| Values | Example |
|---|---|
| Greater than (>) | number in stock > 500 |
| Less than (<) | number in stock < 10 |
| Contains | supplier = Jones |
| Starts with | supplier = F* |
| Ends with | supplier = *g |

## Exam questions

A boat yard stores information about boats and their owners in a database.

**1** Describe, using examples from the boat yard, the difference between a static and dynamic query.　　　　　　[*4 marks*]

**2** Give an example of a simple and complex parameter query that the boat yard could use.　　　　　　[*2 marks*]

## Examiner hints and tips

Think about the following in relation to the above questions.

**Question 1:** The question asks for the difference between the given types of queries. You must clearly state this, but the question also asks for examples related to a boat yard. The examples you give should relate to the queries you are describing.

**Question 2:** Again, the question asks for examples related to a boat yard. Your answer should use the same structure as if inputting the query into a database.

# 6 Applications software used for presentation and communication of data

## 6.1 Characteristics of documents

### Specification reference

**3.1.6a** – describe the characteristics of documents: character, paragraph, sections, frames, headers, footers, footnotes and pages, and how they should be used.

### Keyword

**Alignment:** the positioning of text, for example left, right, centred or justified.

 **Key points to remember**

- All documents have common characteristics that can be used in their production.
- The characteristics used must be based on the needs of the end-users.

## Common characteristics

There are eight characteristics you will need to know about. These are:

- **Characters** – any letter, number or symbol used in a document.

- **Paragraphs** – are generally used when a long document is being created. They are generally defined by the use of a carriage return at the end of the text. The paragraph may have a pre-defined corporate or house style or the style may be defined by the user. The style defines the features of the paragraph text including **alignment**, indentations, line spacing, font size/style and bullets or numbering.

- **Sections** – a portion of a document in which page-formatting options can be set. They can be created when properties such as line numbering, number of columns, or headers and footers need to be changed. Section breaks are inserted to divide the document into sections, allowing each section to be formatted individually.

- **Frames** – an area of a page containing text or graphics. Changes to the content of one frame will not affect the content of another. In a DTP (desktop publishing) package each individual frame can be easily moved or resized. Word processing packages can use frames but are not exclusively frame based. Therefore, the position of each object on the page depends on the position of everything else. For example, if a paragraph or sentence is deleted, everything else moves to take its place.

- **Headers** – text that appears on a document in the top margin of a page.

- **Footers** – text that appears on a document in the bottom margin of a page.

- **Footnotes** – a note commenting on a point in a document, printed at the bottom of the page.

- **Pages** – one side of a document, for example a book, magazine, newspaper or letter.

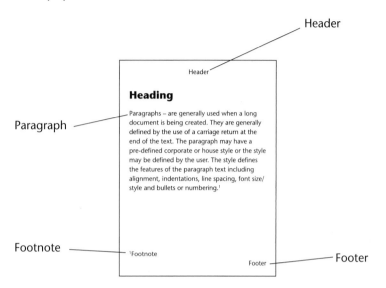

Characteristics of a page

## Exam question

**1** A word processed letter contains a header, a footer and footnotes. Describe a header, a footer and footnotes, giving an example of how each could be used.  [9 marks]

### Examiner hints and tips

Think about the following in relation to the question above.

There are 9 marks available with three characteristics being included in the question. This means that you should make two valid points for each characteristic and provide an example for each (worth 1 mark).

The question infers that the letter has been created using word processing software. It is therefore important that your answer relates to the characteristics as applied to word processing software.

## 6.2 | Mail merge

### Specification reference

**3.1.6b** – describe how word processing and desktop publishing (DTP) software can be used with data from a spreadsheet or database for mail merge, and describe the advantages of using this technique.

 **Keyword**

**Mail merge:** the process of combining information from the data source with a standard document.

### Weblink

**http://office.microsoft.com/en-us/word/HA010349201033.aspx**

An explanation of the mail merge process.

 **Key points to remember**

■ A document created in word processing or DTP software can be combined with information from a spreadsheet or database.

■ This enables personalised letters to be produced.

## ■ Mail merge process

1 A data source is created containing all the information required to be included in the document.

2 The standard document/template is produced including merge fields. These are based on the fields in the spreadsheet or database that is being used as the data source. For example, **Dear <title> <lastname>**.

3 The data source and the standard document/template are linked and merged. The software merges the data by inserting the appropriate fields from the data source.

4 The personalised documents can be sent to a printer or used to create a new file.

### Advantages of mail merge

■ Documents can be produced very quickly.

■ Only one copy of the document needs to be proofread to ensure that all the others are correct.

■ The data source can be used for many different mail merge processes.

■ The standard letter/template can be saved and reused.

### Exam question

**1** Describe the process of mail merge using word processing software and data from a database.                [*4 marks*]

### Examiner hints and tips

Think about the following in relation to the above question.

The question asks about the process of mail merge. However, the mail merge is to be completed using word processing software with the data source being a database. You must therefore focus your answer on these types of software.

**Document formatting**

**3.1.6c** – describe how a document can be reformatted to suit the needs of a given application.

### 🔑 Keyword

**Margins:** the blank space around the edges of the page.

### Weblink

**http://www.baycongroup.com/ wlesson0.htm**

Tutorial on how documents can be reformatted.

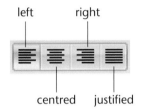

**Text position**

### ⤳ Key point to remember

■ Word processing packages have many features that can help users format the documents being produced to exactly meet their needs.

## ■ Formatting documents

Users can format the attributes of documents including:

■ **Page size** – the size of the page, and the paper to be printed on, can be selected by the user to meet their needs.

■ **Page settings** – **margins** can be set to allow text and graphics to be positioned in the printable area inside the margins. Headers, footers and page numbers can be positioned in the margins.

■ **Page orientation** – the user can select whether the page is to be portrait or landscape.

■ **Text position** – also known as alignment. Alignment can be centre, left, right or justified.

■ **Text size** – can be selected from 8 to 72 points. The text must be sized appropriately to meet the needs of the end user of the document. The text size you are reading is 11 point.

■ **Text style** – text can be selected to be bold, underlined or italic. The font can also be chosen. Some fonts are easy to read like Arial and some are more difficult like Gigi. The font you are reading is ITC Stone Sans.

### Exam question

**1** Identify **four** ways that could be used to make a letter fit onto a single page, without removing any of the content.  [4 marks]

### Examiner hints and tips

Think about the following in relation to the above question.

The question states that none of the content can be removed from the letter. You will need to consider the other ways that could be used, for example making the side margins smaller would enable more text to be fitted on each line of the letter.

# Clip art and thumbnail images

**Specification reference**

**3.1.6d** – discuss the advantages and disadvantages of using clip art images and collections of thumbnail images.

> ## Keywords
>
> **Clip art images:** libraries of pre-drawn pictures/images that can be copied and edited.
>
> **Image library:** a library of ready-to-use images, such as photographs, that can be copied into documents or presentations.

## Key points to remember

- Clip art images are either supplied 'free' with software packages or at a cost from a software manufacturer.
- Thumbnail images from an image library are usually based around a topic and show a preview of an image.

## Clip art images

**Clip art images** can be edited or used as they are.

### Advantages

- Images are readily and immediately available.
- Using clip art can reduce the cost of the design process as a designer does not have to be employed.
- Extra hardware such as scanners and digital cameras do not have to be purchased.

### Disadvantages

- Choice of images is limited to what is available.
- The quality of the images is variable.
- Clip art is not original or unique.
- Clip art images, especially if taken from the internet, may be subject to copyright.

## Exam question

**1** Explain **one** advantage and **one** disadvantage of using an image of a computer from an image library. [*4 marks*]

## Examiner hints and tips

Think about the following in relation to the above question.

The question refers to a computer. You will need to tailor your answer to focus on the use of this type of image. You must include both an advantage and a disadvantage. Generic answers may not gain many marks.

## Thumbnail images

When an image in an **image library** is clicked then the actual image is shown.

### Advantages

- Many images can be viewed at the same time.
- Images that are alike can be grouped together.
- Descriptions can be added to the images so that they can be searched for.

### Disadvantages

- The quality of the images may be poor.
- If the image library holds a large number of images then it can take a long time to load an individual image.
- It is not always possible to tell whether the actual image is of a better quality or a larger size than the preview or thumbnail image.

## 6.5 Graphic libraries

### Specification reference

**3.1.6f** – describe the advantages and disadvantages of using graphic libraries and their use in the following applications: kitchen design, cartography and network design.

### Keywords

**Graphic library:** a collection of graphics relating to a specified topic.

**Cartography:** the art or technique of making maps.

### Weblink

**http://www.map-symbol.com/ sym_lib.htm**

An example of a graphic library that can be used for cartography.

### Key point to remember

■ Graphic libraries provide symbols and images related to a specific topic or application.

## Graphic libraries

**Graphic libraries** are specialist applications developed with the involvement of manufacturers and professional bodies.

### Advantages

- Industry-standard symbols are available.
- The symbols will be recognised throughout the world.

### Disadvantages

- May be difficult to keep up-to-date.
- New components may not be available immediately.
- Components may be included that are not used or available.

## Applications

**Kitchen design** – will include standard symbols for cupboards and kitchen appliances (cookers, dishwashers, etc.), which are used when planning and designing a kitchen layout.

**Cartography** – will contain symbols used by the Ordnance Survey so maps created for a specific purpose, such as a cycle track, will use the symbols used on standard maps.

**Network design** – contain industry-standard symbols for the main components needed in a network, for example servers, routers and cabling.

### Exam question

1 Explain how a graphic library could be used to produce a map for a driving competition.
[4 marks]

### Examiner hints and tips

Think about the following in relation to the question opposite.

The question refers to a driving competition. You will need to tailor your answer to focus on this type of event. Generic answers may not gain many marks.

You should also provide examples of the types of symbols that could be included on the map and consider the size of the map that would be given to the competitors.

# 6.6 Vector and bitmap graphics

## Specification reference

**3.1.6e –** describe the differences between vector and bitmap graphics and evaluate their suitability for given applications.

## Keywords

**Vector graphics:** graphics saved as geometric equations.

**Bitmap graphics:** graphics stored as pixels.

## Weblink

**http://www.sketchpad.net/basics1.htm**

An explanation of the differences between vector and bitmap graphics.

## Key points to remember

- Graphics can be stored as vector or bitmap graphics.
- Vector and bitmap graphics have different characteristics.
- Vector and bitmap graphics are used in different applications.

## Differences between vector and bitmap graphics

The main differences between **vector** and **bitmap graphics** are shown in the table below:

| Vector | Bitmap |
|---|---|
| Can be resized or rescaled with no loss of definition. | When resized there is a lowering of image quality: can become pixellated. |
| File size is relatively small compared with a bitmap graphic file. | File size can be very large as each pixel in the image has to be saved individually. |
| Every component of the graphic is described by its features (length, colour, thickness, etc.). | The components of the graphic are only stored as pixels with their attributes. |
| Can be grouped. | Cannot be grouped. |
| Cannot be compressed. | Can be compressed. |
| The processing power required to display a vector-based graphic on display equipment is high. | The screen resolution of the display equipment can affect the display of the colours used in a bitmap graphic. |
| Each individual element can be edited independently. | Each pixel can be edited separately. |
| Can be produced using a word-processing package. | Can be used to make subtle changes to complex images, such as photographs. |

Image at 100%

Image at 400%

**Vector graphic**

Image at 100%

Image at 400%

**Bitmap graphic**

# Use of vector and bitmap graphics

**Vector graphics** – used in design and **CAD** packages. They enable users, such as architects and designers, to change size, perspective and proportions of components in their drawings.

Vector graphics are essential when CAD/**CAM** systems are being used. This is when the whole or part of the graphic is being used as the basis for instructions to automated machines.

**Bitmap graphics** – produced when a scanner or camera is used. Most clipart is saved as bitmap graphics. This means that the clip art can sometimes be edited and changed to meet the needs of the user – assuming it is copyright free! Bitmap graphics can be saved as different file types including BMP, GIF and JPEG.

## Exam questions

1 Describe **two** differences between vector and bitmap graphics. [4 marks]

2 An engineer can save his plans as a vector or bitmap graphic. Identify, justifying your choice, which format he should use. [5 marks]

## Examiner hints and tips

Think about the following in relation to the above questions.

**Question 1:** One of the differences between bitmap and vector graphics is that bitmap graphics pixellate on enlargement. An answer which states that pixellation occurs when the bitmap graphic is resized would be too vague as resizing can mean making smaller as well as larger.

**Question 2:** The question refers to an engineer. You will need to tailor your answer to focus on an engineer. Generic answers may not gain many marks.

# 6.7 Features of presentation software

**Specification reference**

**3.1.6g** – describe the features of presentation software: text, images, sound, video, animation, slide transition, hyperlinks, hotspots, buttons.

### ⤢ Key points to remember

- Presentation software has a range of features that can be used to enhance a presentation.
- All features used must meet the needs of the audience and not detract from the message.

## ■ Features of presentation software

### Keyword

**Presentation software:** software used to create presentations of slides containing text and graphics. Sound and visual effects can also be included.

**Presentation software** has a range of features that can be used to enhance the presentation and deliver the message to the target audience:

- **Text** – the style and size of text should meet the needs of the audience. They should enable the audience to clearly read the text on each slide. Fancy text should be avoided.

- **Images** – images can help convey the message or can be used as an aide-memoire by the presenter. The number of images and graphics used on each slide should be kept to a minimum and they should be of a size that can be clearly seen by the audience. Who owns the copyright of the images should be considered.

- **Sound** – includes speech and music. Sound effects can be set with animation effects, for example clapping when a new slide appears. Sound files can be pre-existing files, such as a company advertising jingle, downloaded from the internet or recorded to meet the specific needs of a particular presentation.

- **Video** – video clips can be inserted into a presentation. A video can be set up to play automatically or on a prompt from the presenter.

- **Animation** – animation effects are visual effects that can be added to text and objects, such as a chart or picture, to control the way that objects appear on a slide. Animation can be used to emphasise important points, control the flow of information within the presentation and add interest.

- **Slide transition** – transition effects govern how the presentation software moves from slide to slide. They can be used to make the presentation more interesting, applied to one or all of the slides or combined with sound.

# Features of a presentation slide

- **Hyperlinks** – coloured and underlined text or a graphic which, when clicked, takes the user to a file, a location in a file or an HTML page on the internet or an intranet. A hyperlink can take the form of any object the creator wants.

- **Hotspots** – a graphic or text which produces an action when clicked. They are usually used to take the user to another page in the presentation.

- **Buttons** – can be used to take the user from one slide to the next. They make the presentation interactive by allowing the user to select the slides viewed or change the order of viewing.

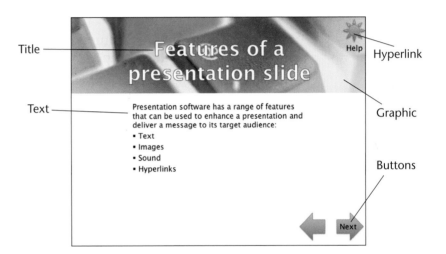

## Exam questions

**1** Explain how sound and video could be used in a presentation, giving an example for each. [6 marks]

**2** Describe how a user could navigate a presentation using buttons. [3 marks]

### Examiner hints and tips

Think about the following in relation to the above questions.

**Question 1:** There are two features given in the question so each feature must be worth 3 marks. An example is asked for, so 1 of the 3 marks is allocated for this. If a scenario is included in the question then the example must relate to this.

**Question 2:** The focus of this question is on buttons and how they can be used to help a user. Your answer must focus on buttons – if you give an answer related to other navigation aids then you will gain no marks.

# Delivering a presentation

## Specification reference

**3.1.6h** – compare delivering a presentation using printed acetate and using a computer and projector describing the advantages and disadvantages of each.

### 🔑 Keyword

**Presentation:** a set of slides that can be presented to an audience on a large monitor or projected onto a screen.

## Weblink

**http://www.oucs.ox.ac.uk/ltg/ resources/archive/ppt.xml. ID=delivers**

A guide to the differences between creating a presentation for acetates and a computer/projector.

**Overhead projector**

## 🗘 Key points to remember

- Presentations can be given using a computer and projector or by using printed acetate and an overhead projector.
- Presentation software can be used to create and print acetates and create presentations.

## Computer and projector

### Advantages

- A wide range of features can be used, with slides being shown in the order the presenter wants.
- The presentation can be saved and edited.
- The quality of the slides does not diminish with use.

### Disadvantages

- Features can be overused, for example too many sounds.
- A computer and projector have a large initial cost.
- Software is needed to edit the slides in real time.
- If there is a power cut the presentation cannot be shown.

## Printed acetate and overhead projector (OHP)

### Advantages

- Slides can be annotated to explain/highlight points.
- An OHP is relatively cheap and rarely goes wrong.
- If there is a power cut the slides can be read by the presenter.

### Disadvantages

- Special features such as sound and interactivity cannot be used.
- It is difficult to jump to an out of sequence slide.
- If a slide needs to be edited then a new slide will need to be printed.
- The quality of slides can deteriorate with use.

## Exam question

**1** Compare the use of a computer and projector with the use of printed acetate and an OHP. **[3 marks]**

## Examiner hints and tips

Think about the following in relation to the question opposite.

The question asks for a comparison. This means you should use both methods for each point you make. There are 3 marks available so you should be giving three comparisons. You must give full explanations for each method and not simply state 'and the other does not'.

## 6.9 Navigation methods

### Specification reference

**3.1.6i** – compare and give advantages and disadvantages of different modes of navigation (automatic and manual transition) and identify and give examples of when the use of each method is more suitable.

**Keyword**

**Slide transition:** how presentation software moves from slide to slide.

### Weblink

**http://www2.essex.ac.uk/cs/ documentation/use/PowerPoint/p-point.htm**

A guide to the differences between automatic and manual transition.

### Key point to remember

■ A slide show can be presented using manual or automatic transition methods.

## ▉ Manual transition

■ Involves some form of action from the presenter to move on to the next slide.

■ If the slide contains a number of items, then each item can be displayed manually. For example, a numbered list can be displayed one point at a time.

■ Usually used when a presentation is given by a speaker to an audience.

■ The presenter is able to control when each slide, or item, is displayed.

■ The pace can be tailored to meet the needs of the audience.

## ▉ Automatic transition

■ The presentation is set up to run automatically with no intervention required to move on to the next slide.

■ Timings can be changed but these must be set to give the audience sufficient time to read each slide before moving to the next one.

■ The presentation can also be set to restart as soon as it has finished.

■ A presenter is not needed.

■ Not suitable for verbal presentations as the presenter may struggle to keep pace with the presentation.

### Exam questions

**1** Describe **two** advantages of using manual transition for a presentation. [*4 marks*]

**2** A presentation is to be shown in a dentist's waiting room. Identify, justifying your choice, the most appropriate transition method.
[*3 marks*]

### Examiner hints and tips

Think about the following in relation to the questions opposite.

**Question 1:** This asks for two advantages of manual transition. You should ensure that you focus your answer on manual transition and provide a full description.

**Question 2:** This asks for the identification of a transition method in a dentist's waiting room. The justification you give must apply to this scenario.

## 6.10 Presentation structure

### Specification reference

**3.1.6j** – describe nonlinear and hierarchical presentations giving the advantages and disadvantages of each. Identify and give examples of where each may be more suitable.

### Key points to remember

- A presentation is made up of a number of slides.
- There are three main structures which a presentation can take.
- The structure provides a route through the presentation.

## ■ Different presentation structures

The structure of the presentation needs to meet the needs of the content of the presentation and the target audience.

There are three main structures:

- Linear
- Nonlinear
- Hierarchical

**Linear structure** – this is where the slides follow on in a consecutive manner. One slide links to the slide immediately after it and there is no facility to jump to other slides within the presentation.

**Nonlinear structure** – this is where slides can be accessed in any order. This structure gives the presenter the option to 'jump' over slides to individual or groups of slides.

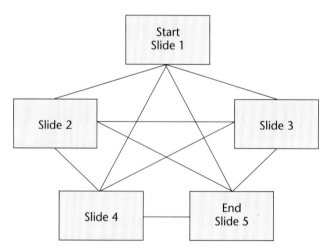

**Non-linear presentation structure**

**Hierarchical structure** – this is where different options can be selected from each slide.

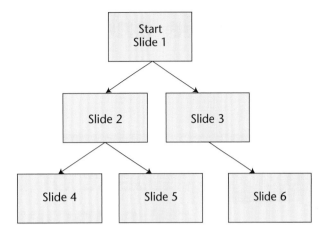

Hierarchical presentation structure

## Advantages and disadvantages

| | Advantages | Disadvantages |
|---|---|---|
| Nonlinear | • The presenter can show the slides in any order dependent on the needs of the audience.<br>• The presentation can be tailored to meet the needs of the audience.<br>• The same presentation can be customised to different audiences by showing slides in a different sequence. | • The structure can be very complicated to create.<br>• The layout of the slides may become over-complicated with too many navigation buttons. |
| Hierarchical | • The options are set up when the presentation is created so a pre-determined order is followed.<br>• Options can be selected to meet the needs of the audience. | • The user cannot jump to another slide that is out of sequence.<br>• The user may not find the slide/information required if it is not in sequence. |

## Exam questions

1 Describe **two** advantages and **one** disadvantage of the nonlinear presentation structure.
[6 marks]

2 Identify **one** situation where the use of a hierarchical presentation structure would be appropriate.
[1 mark]

## Examiner hints and tips

Think about the following in relation to the above questions.

**Question 1:** The focus of this question is on the nonlinear presentation structure. You must provide two advantages and one disadvantage relating to this to be awarded full marks. The table above will help you answer this question, although you may think of alternative answers.

**Question 2:** The question refers to the hierarchical presentation structure. You will need to provide identification directly related to this structure.

# The role and impact of ICT

# Impact of ICT and future developments

### Specification references

**3.1.7a** – discuss the impact of ICT on society, organisations and individuals.
**3.1.7b** – discuss possible future developments in ICT and their impact on the following application areas: transport, medicine, the disabled, education, entertainment, shopping, marketing and communication.

### Keyword

**Teleworking:** the use of technology that allows an employee to work from home – the use of computers, internet, mobile phones, web cams, etc. to replace being in the office.

### Weblink

**http://www.wired.co.uk/**

Up-to-date news and discussions on ICT.

### Key points to remember

- Look at page 97 – the discussion is as important as the content.
- Read newspapers, watch television news programmes – keep up to date with developments in ICT.

## ◼ Society, organisations and individuals

This section is concerned with how ICT is used and the positive and negative impacts that it has on society, organisations and individuals.

**Society** – topics include the depersonalisation of devices, leading to less communication between individuals, the increase in accessibility to illicit information (for example, pornography) and criminal activities (for example, copyright theft). Is the increased reliance on computers and technology good or bad? Could we exist without mobile phones, the internet and computers? Wider topics might include increased leisure time, city centres becoming deserted, constant expectation to work (even when away from work), technology for disadvantaged groups and the deskilling of a generation.

**Organisations** – these are the businesses that use ICT. Topics include **teleworking** which can result in less need for business premises, and employees working longer hours and having less control. Another topic is the use of ICT in management information systems, for example providing information to make decisions and creating simulations. Increased communication between employees through the use of mobile phones and webcams has both positive and negative implications for organisations. The type and variety of jobs available and the changing structure of organisations as a direct consequence of the introduction of ICT is another area of discussion.

**Individuals** – these are the people who use ICT. Issues include lack of privacy and over-dependence on technological devices and information resources such as Wikipedia. The impact of ICT on the family and the use of technology at home is also an area for discussion.

# Future developments in ICT

There are constant changes to ICT – hardware, software and how the technology is used. The specification identifies the key areas of transport, medicine, the disabled, education, entertainment, shopping, marketing and communication. You should research these topics, focusing on the areas of each topic you are familiar with and would wish to use in your answer. Some ideas have been given below for each topic – you would need to develop positive and negative impacts and consequences of these to get full marks.

**Transport** – route planning and GPS, automatic driving systems, computer technology to judge distances and apply accelerator and brake, in transport entertainment systems, transport booking systems and environmental issues.

**Medicine** – administrative issues such as patient records, treatment files and accessibility to information. Also advances in surgery with new equipment, remote surgery and diagnostics (including expert systems, technology for body part replacement and 3D imaging).

**The disabled** – hardware to allow access to the same ICT as others and removal of prejudice with communication via the internet, internet shopping and virtual shopping centres.

**Education** – administration as well as teaching tools.

**Entertainment and communication** – portable devices, immersion technology, multi-sensory approaches (for example, sound, light and movement in chairs, mobile phones and video phones).

**Shopping and marketing** – internet shopping, data mining to identify purchasing trends and new methods of advertising.

**Keyword**

**Future developments in ICT:** these include hardware, software and different uses for technology. They do not have to be futuristic but must be recent.

## Weblinks

**http://news.bbc.co.uk/1/hi/technology/default.stm**

**http://news.bbc.co.uk/1/hi/programmes/click_online/**

Links: for keeping up to date with developments.

## Exam questions

**1** Discuss the impact of ICT on transport.  [*11 marks*]

**2** Discuss the impact of portable devices on individuals.  [*11 marks*]

## Examiner hints and tips

Think about the following in relation to the above questions.

**Question 1:** Examples can include route planning, GPS, environmental and automatic controls, and diagnostics. You could also discuss issues of comfort, entertainment and remote working whilst using transport.

**Question 2:** Answers can include music or video players, hand held games, computers, mobile phones or any other mobile device.

## 7.2  Legal aspects of ICT

**Specification reference**

**3.1.7c** – discuss the main aspects, purpose and implications of the Data Protection Act (1998), Computer Misuse Act (1990), Copyright, Designs and Patents Act (1988), Regulation of Investigatory Powers Act (2000), Electronic Communications Act (2000) and Freedom of Information Act (2000) and subsequent changes/updates.

**Keyword**

**Data subject:** an individual who is the subject of personal data – they must be living and identifiable.

### Weblink

**http://www.ico.gov.uk/for_the_public/topic_specific_guides.aspx**

Guides to data protection from the Information Commissioner.

### Key points to remember

■ Be careful not to confuse the different Acts.

■ Some Acts relate to the individual, some to the company and some are for the benefit of the country.

## The Data Protection Act (1998)

The Data Protection Act was set up to protect individuals from organisations. Certain rights were laid down in the Act for the benefit of the individual. The six main rights include the right to subject access, the right to prevent processing likely to cause damage or distress, the right to prevent processing for the purposes of direct marketing, rights in relation to automated decision making, the right to compensation if damage and distress is suffered by the act being contravened and the right to rectify, block or erase incorrect data.

The Data Protection Act has eight principles that must be followed by the organisation, summarised below:

1 Personal data shall be processed fairly and lawfully.

2 Personal data shall be obtained only for one or more specified and lawful purposes.

3 Personal data shall be adequate, relevant and not excessive in relation to the purpose.

4 Personal data shall be accurate and, where necessary, kept up to date.

5 Personal data shall not be kept for longer than is necessary for the purpose it is required.

6 Personal data shall be processed in accordance with the rights of **data subjects**.

7 Personal data must be kept secure.

8 Personal data shall not be transferred outside the European Union, unless that country ensures an adequate level of protection for the rights and freedoms of data subjects.

## Computer Misuse Act (1990)

The Computer Misuse Act was introduced to protect data held by companies from hackers. It has four main provisions:

1 Unauthorised access to computer material.

2 Unauthorised access with intent to commit or facilitate the commission of further offences.

3 Unauthorised acts with intent to impair, or with recklessness as to impairing, operation of a computer.

4 Making, supplying or obtaining articles for use in computer misuse offences.

Weblink

http://www.networkworld.com/news/64452_05-17-1999.html

Explanation of public key encryption.

# Copyright, Designs and Patents Act (1988)

The Copyright, Designs and Patents Act makes it illegal to steal or create unauthorised copies of software. It also covers manuals, books, CDs and music.

# Regulation of Investigatory Powers Act (2000)

The Regulation of Investigatory Powers Act was introduced to address concerns about the use and misuse of communication interception techniques by public and private organisations. The Act allows for the lawful interception of telecommunications and postal and digital communications. The Act makes it a criminal offence to monitor communications without lawful authority. Communications being telephone calls, emails, post, etc.

To be lawful, 'the interception has to be by or with the consent of a person carrying on a business, for purposes relevant to that person's business, and using that business's own telecommunications system'.

# Electronic Communications Act (2000)

The Electronic Communications Act is in two main parts:

- **Cryptography** service providers – this allows the government to set up a register of 'approved cryptography suppliers'.

- Facilitation of electronic commerce data storage – this recognises digital signatures, which are now admissible in law.

# Freedom of Information Act (2000)

The Freedom of Information Act deals with access to official information, that is being able to find out information on any topic from any public authority. It applies to all public authorities.

The Act allows anyone to make a request for information they think a public authority holds. The authorities have 20 working days to comply with your request.

## Exam questions

1 Identify **four** of the rights of individuals under the Data Protection Act (1998). [4 marks]

2 Describe **two** benefits to the company of the Regulation of Investigatory Powers Act (2000). [4 marks]

## Examiner hints and tips

Think about the following in relation to the questions opposite.

**Question 1:** Do not give any of the eight principles; the question is about the rights of individuals.

**Question 2:** The answer must include two benefits for the company, not the user. Identify two benefits and then give an example of each to gain full marks.

# 7.3 Combating ICT crime and protecting ICT systems

## Specification reference

**3.1.7d** – explain methods for combating ICT crime and protecting ICT systems: physical security, firewalls, backup, encryption, biometric security, software patches/updates, 'anti-virus' and anti-spyware software, access rights, auditing, education of users, user IDs, passwords and methods for ensuring passwords remain effective.

### Keywords

**ICT crime:** a criminal act that involves the use of a computer. This includes the use of a computer to hack and copy music and films. Also known as cybercrime.

**Biometric:** the use of unique and identifiable physical traits to confirm identity, such as iris, fingerprint and voice.

### Weblinks

**http://www.itsecurity. com/features/ top-10-famous-hackers-042407/**

Ten famous computer hackers.

**http://www.time.com/time/nation/ article/0,8599,1902073,00.html**

A brief history of cybercrime.

## Key points to remember

- There are two methods for protecting ICT systems – physical and logical.
- Preventing physical access to the data is not the same as protecting the data.

## ■ Physical methods

Physical methods prevent a person from getting access to a computer in person. Methods to protect against physical access include having security guards on the door and giving each employee a pass that the guard checks. You could have an automatic door that responds to a pass given to each employee. The computers could be kept in locked rooms with only specific people given access to them. Security cameras could monitor corridors and rooms.

Physical methods also include the positioning of the screen and keyboard. If the machine is in an open access area, like a reception, then positioning the screen and keyboard so they cannot be seen by the public are sensible precautions.

Increasingly, **biometric** measures such as scanning a person's iris or fingerprint are being used to provide physical security.

**Biometric iris scanner**

## ■ Logical methods

Logical methods are computer based and are applied by a system administrator. They include usernames and passwords, access rights and user groups. Other logical methods include screensaver passwords, firewalls and anti-virus software as well as logging and analysing actions.

When you log on to a computer system you are asked for two pieces of information, user ID and password.

**Login screen**

A user ID is a unique identifier for a user, identifying who the user is to the system. The user ID can be allocated to groups and those groups can have access rights and programs allocated to them. According to which user group they belong to, a user might only be allowed to read a file, while other users might have access to edit or delete. The user ID can also restrict the user to only logging onto certain machines or at certain times of the day. The network manager can see the user ID to log what the user is doing.

A password is a method of restricting access. Unless you know the password you cannot perform tasks. When used in conjunction with a user ID, the password authenticates who the user is – that they are who the user ID says they are. This assumes that only the user knows the password.

Passwords are a weak link in any system. The network manager can apply controls to the password to make them harder for other users to find out. Such controls might include using a minimum number of characters, using a combination of numbers and letters, not using a word in the dictionary, changing passwords monthly, not allowing previous passwords to be used, only allowing three password attempts, forcing the password to be impersonal and educating users.

Preventative methods for combating ICT crime include the threat of legal action and ensuring that software is kept up to date. Keeping anti-spyware, anti-spam and anti-virus software up to date is just as important.

Other methods that can be employed to make it more difficult for data to be stolen and used include auditing, firewalls and encryption.

## Exam questions

**1** Identify **three** controls that can be placed on passwords and, for each, give an example of how it can enable the password to remain effective.
[4 marks]

**2** Describe **two** physical methods that can prevent data being stolen. [3 marks]

### Examiner hints and tips

Think about the following in relation to the questions opposite.

**Question 1:** These are not rules for the user to follow but controls that can be placed on a password and enforced by a network manager.

**Question 2:** You need to make sure you cover physical methods only.

### Specification reference

**3.1.7e** – describe the advantages and disadvantages of networking computers.

### Keywords

**Standalone:** has no network connection to other internal computers – may still have an internet connection.

**Networked:** two or more computers within a company that are connected together and can exchange data.

### Weblink

**http://compnetworking.about.com/**

The basics of computer networking.

**Networking computers in an office**

### ⬈ Key point to remember

■ Advantages and disadvantages apply to different users – management, end users, customers and network managers.

## Advantages

The advantages of networking include the sharing of peripherals. This reduces maintenance for the network manager and reduces overall running costs. Data can also be shared amongst several people in a team allowing them to work on the same document. The advantages to the network manager and management include controlling access to data through user IDs and access rights, monitoring and logging the resources used by individuals and controlling backup and virus checking from a central location. The latter is also an advantage for the users as it removes responsibility. On a network the users can communicate with email systems and an intranet can disseminate useful information. This is an advantage for all.

## Disadvantages

The disadvantages of networking are, for the majority, concerned with restricting the work that can be done. If a network component fails then work cannot be done. If a virus is introduced into a single station it can spread throughout the network. If the network is particularly busy, it may have a detrimental effect on the work that the user can do.

## Exam questions

1 Describe **two** advantages to the network manager of networking computers.                                    [4 marks]

2 Describe **two** problems for end users that could be caused by networking computers.                            [4 marks]

### Examiner hints and tips

Think about the following in relation to the above questions.

**Question 1:** The focus is the network manager and advantages. Both of these should be evident in your answer.

**Question 2:** Although the disadvantages are generic, your answer should be tailored to include specific disadvantages for the end user.

# 7.5 Standards in ICT

**Specification reference**

**3.1.7f** – explain why standards are required and the impact of different organisations and networks having different standards.

**Keyword**

**Protocol:** the set of standard rules for data representation, signalling, authentication and error detection required to send information over a communications channel.

**Weblink**

http://www.protocols.com/hot.htm

Protocols and standards.

## Key points to remember

- Protocols govern the language of communication.
- Standardisation is about how data can be exchanged.

## ■ Standards

A network is two or more computers connected together so that they can communicate. Without communication between the computers and the peripherals they cannot exchange information – this might be printer data, files or password authentication.

In order for the computers to communicate they need to be talking the same language. This means that they need to be running the same protocol or standard.

A **protocol** is a set of communication rules. It governs:

- the format of the message
- the type of error checking to be used
- any compression
- how the sending device indicates it has finished sending
- how the receiving device indicates that it has received the message.

If computers and organisations are not communicating using the same standard then data transfer will not be possible, or if it does occur, is likely to be incorrect.

---

### Exam questions

**1** Explain the impact on an organisation of having its computers running different protocols. [4 marks]

**2** Explain why standards are required. [4 marks]

---

### Examiner hints and tips

Think about the following in relation to the above questions.

**Question 1:** Your answer should be about the problems caused by a lack of standardisation. There is some crossover with section 3.1.2a of the specification.

**Question 2:** Your answer needs to focus on communication and the consequences of not using the same standards.

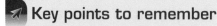

# 7.6 Health problems

## Specification reference

**3.1.7g** – describe health problems related to working with ICT: repetitive strain injury, carpal tunnel syndrome, ulnar neuritis, deep vein thrombosis, eyesight defects, fatigue, backache and stress.

## Key points to remember

■ The description and the cause are two different things and will be asked in two different questions.

■ Health problems can be underlying and exacerbated by computer use.

## Keyword

**Repetitive:** completing the same actions with no break between them – pressing the same keys or moving the body in the same directions.

### Weblinks

**http://heheli.com/business/top-4-health-problems-caused-by-computer-use/**

The top four computer health problems.

**http://menshealth.about.com/cs/workhealth/a/computers.htm**

Are computers damaging your health?

# ■ Health problems

There are several problems that can be caused by using computers for a long period of time. They are usually related to posture. Some examples are given below. The causes given are not the only ones.

| Health risk | Description | Cause |
|---|---|---|
| Deep vein thrombosis (DVT) | Blood clot, usually in the leg | Sitting in a chair that puts pressure on the back of the knees |
| Repetitive strain injury (RSI) | Chronic pain experienced in the arms, shoulder or back | Repetitive actions, poor posture while working, maintaining a fixed forced position |
| Carpal tunnel syndrome (CTS) | Pressure on the median nerve in the wrist | Repeated wrist movements such as typing |
| Ulnar neuritis (cubital tunnel syndrome) | Compression of the ulnar nerve in the elbow | Leaning on the elbow for prolonged periods of time |
| Eyesight | Hazy vision, tired eyes | Looking at a monitor for long periods of time, dehydration of the eyes |
| Back pain/ache | Muscle spasms | Poor posture, sitting in the same position, forced position |
| Fatigue | Tiredness and lethargy | Continued periods of mental work |
| Stress | State of mental strain | Overwork or software/hardware not doing what you expect |

# Posture

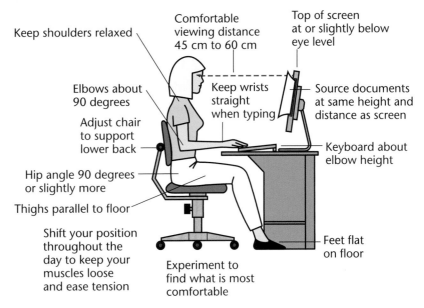

Keep shoulders relaxed

Comfortable viewing distance 45 cm to 60 cm

Top of screen at or slightly below eye level

Elbows about 90 degrees

Keep wrists straight when typing

Source documents at same height and distance as screen

Adjust chair to support lower back

Keyboard about elbow height

Hip angle 90 degrees or slightly more

Thighs parallel to floor

Shift your position throughout the day to keep your muscles loose and ease tension

Experiment to find what is most comfortable

Feet flat on floor

Posture is very important when dealing with health problems. Many are caused by incorrect posture or incorrect positioning of office furniture and computer hardware.

# Repetitive actions

Other health problems are related to repetitive actions – these include repetitive strain injury (RSI) and carpal tunnel syndrome (CTS). The impact of repetitive actions can be lessened by correct posture and correct positioning of office furniture and computer hardware.

## Exam questions

**1** Describe **two** health problems caused by incorrect posture.

[*4 marks*]

**2** Describe **two** health problems caused by repetitive actions.

[*4 marks*]

### Examiner hints and tips

Think about the following in relation to the questions above.

**Question 1:** The description of the problem should not include the cause – you should describe the symptoms of each health problem.

**Question 2:** Not all health problems are caused by repetitive actions – you need to think about those that are.

## 7.7 Safety problems

### Specification reference

**3.1.7h** – describe safety problems related to working with ICT: trailing wires, risk of fire and electrocution, unsecured equipment, food and drink and proximity to water.

### Key points to remember

- Safety problems have immediate impacts.
- Health and safety are different.

| Safety hazard | Description | Risk |
|---|---|---|
| Trailing wires | Wires from computers trailing onto the floor | Can trip over the wire or fall over |
| Overheating of computers | Overheating of computers can cause them to catch fire | Fire |
| Overloading of plug sockets | Fire can break out slowly or cause an explosion | Fire |
| Close proximity of water and electricity | Water and electricity can cause electrocution | Electrocution |
| Bare wires | When touched, can cause electrocution | Heart can stop or even death in severe cases |
| Unstable surfaces and office furniture | Falling computer hardware, or falling from furniture | Injury from falling computer hardware, or from falling from furniture |
| Food and drink | Liquids can cause shorting and lead to fire. Crumbs from food are a fire hazard | Electrocution and fire |

### Keyword

**Work safety:** ensuring that the work environment is free from risk and that all equipment being used is appropriate. Making sure that correct techniques are followed and a culture of safe working is promoted.

### Weblink

**http://www.workplacesafetyadvice. co.uk/**

Advice on work place safety.

## Exam questions

**1** Describe **two** safety problems caused by malfunctioning equipment. [4 marks]

**2** Describe **two** safety problems caused by incorrect fitting of equipment. [4 marks]

### Examiner hints and tips

Think about the following in relation to the above questions.

**Question 1:** Your answer should be narrowed down to things that can break and cause a safety problem.

**Question 2:** Your answer should be related to electrical equipment, desks and wires – items that are fitted into an office/room for computer use.

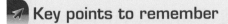

## 7.8 Avoiding health and safety problems

### Specification reference

**3.1.7i** – describe appropriate measures for avoiding health and safety problems.

### Key points to remember

- Using 'regular breaks' in an answer is not acceptable – you should use 'five minute break every hour'.
- Using 'comfortable chair' in an answer is not acceptable – you should use 'adjustable chair'.

### Keyword

**Adjustable chair:** a chair that can be adjusted in height and tilt, supports the lower back, has five casters, a swivel mechanism, a leading edge that tilts towards the floor, arm rests at 90 degrees and appropriate seat depth.

### Weblink

**http://www.voluntarymatters1and2.org/organisation/it/more_depth/health_safety.html**

The health and safety implications of using computers.

## Solving health problems

| Heath problem | Prevention |
|---|---|
| Deep vein thrombosis (DVT) | Using correct posture when sitting and standing up and moving around |
| Repetitive strain injury (RSI) | Using correct workstation, keyboard rests, foot stools and adjustable chairs and taking frequent breaks from continuous activity |
| Carpal tunnel syndrome (CTS) | Avoiding repetitive actions and taking frequent breaks |
| Ulnar neuritis | Using wrist rests and adjustable height chairs and setting correct desk height |
| Eye strain | Drinking plenty of fluids and using correctly adjusted, flicker-free monitors |
| Back pain/ache | Using correct posture and adjustable chairs |
| Fatigue | Taking a five minute break every hour and varying the work |
| Stress | Taking a five minute break every hour and appropriate training |

## Solving safety problems

| Safety problem | Prevention |
|---|---|
| Trailing wires | Cable management systems to cover wires |
| Fire | Adequate ventilation of computers and clear space around equipment; not overloading plug sockets; correct number of sockets on a breaker; correct fire extinguisher ($CO_2$) for electrical fires |
| Electrocution | No drinking near computers; no water near computers; all wires to be frequently checked and repaired |
| Unstable surfaces and chairs | All surfaces to be stable before equipment is placed on them |

## Exam questions

1 Identify **two** safety problems and give different solutions to prevent them. [*4 marks*]

2 Identify **two** health problems and give solutions to prevent them. [*4 marks*]

### Examiner hints and tips

Think about the following in relation to the questions opposite.

Health is long term, safety is short term. The solutions must be different and specific – use 'five minute break every hour' rather than 'regular breaks' and 'adjustable chair' rather than 'comfortable chair'.

# Examination techniques

## Types of examination questions and how to answer them

If you look at some past examination papers, you will see that the questions include a keyword such as 'identify' or 'describe'. You must recognise these keywords and respond to them correctly. The keywords determine how you should structure your answer and what you are required to do to be allocated marks.

The keywords used are described and explained below.

### State or identify

In this example, you have to write a single word or phrase. These questions are worth 1 mark each.

> **Example**
>
> **1** A database package holds data in fields.
>
> State **three** data types, other than text, commonly used in databases.

Your answers only need to be single words. For example:

*Boolean, Integer, Date*

### Describe

These types of questions are moving to a higher level of difficulty. These questions are usually worth at least two marks. You need to provide an answer that matches the question asked, using the given context. As a rule of thumb, try to give an example related to the scenario. Remember a good description might earn extra marks in some questions. Take your time in thinking about these questions and preparing your answer.

In this example, you need to give an identification and then expand on what you have identified – this is known as exemplification. Wherever possible, using an example related to the context is a good idea.

> **Example**
>
> **2** Spreadsheets are used for modelling situations.
>
> Describe the features of spreadsheet applications which enable them to be used for modelling.

You need to first identify the feature that you are going to talk about and then give some more information. For example:

*Recalculation – this is where one value is changed and all linked values are updated.*

*Functions – these are built into the spreadsheet and can be used to assist in the calculations.*

## Explain

In this example, it requires you to provide advantages. Your answer should provide reasons for these being valid. Answers must also use continuous prose.

### Example

> **3** Explain the advantages of using text for storing house numbers.

Your answer needs to include a reason, followed by the advantages of that reason:

*House numbers can be numbers, such as 2 or 3, but they can also include letters, such as 212B or 53C. Text allows both types to be stored in the same field instead of using different fields.*

## Compare

In this example, you will need to identify a feature to compare and then apply that feature to both things being compared. If you are asked to compare you must include both sides of the comparison.

To help structure your answer you can make use of a writing frame.

### Example

> **4** Compare the use of automatic and manual transition in a slideshow when teaching a lesson.

Your answer will need to identify a feature and give an explanation of how automatic and manual transition deal with that feature. The writing frame below has been used to ensure a proper comparison is made:

| Feature | Manual | Automatic |
|---|---|---|
| Questions from the class | Can pause at any time | Have to wait until the end |
| Skipping slides | Can skip through slides if not required | Have to go through every slide |
| Location of teacher | Has to be at the computer unless they have a remote mouse | Can be anywhere, not even in the room |

You then need to write your answer using continuous prose. Use words such as 'whereas', 'and' and 'but' to help you in your comparison.

> *With manual transition you can take questions from the class and pause the presentation. Whereas with automatic you have to wait to the end and the moment might have passed.*
>
> *With manual transition you can skip through slides if you are running out of time or if they have already been covered in discussion. Whereas with automatic you cannot skip slides but have to run through every slide at the programmed speed.*
>
> *With manual transition unless you have a remote mouse you need to be where the computer is that is running the presentation, whereas with automatic you can be anywhere in the room; in fact as it runs itself you do not even have to be in the room.*

This is a high level of response and requires considerable writing to gain full marks.

## Evaluate

In this example, you need to examine the subject and decide how much, or how little, the value of something is worth, arriving at a judgement.

### Example

**5** Evaluate the use of vector graphics for use in cartography.

You need to look at the benefits and limitations of using vector graphics and then draw a conclusion, with a reason as to whether they are suitable or not.

> *Maps come in different scales and vector graphics can be increased in size with no loss of definition of the image. If there are pictures of locations on the map then vector graphics will not be able to give much detail. On a large map there will be a lot of detail and because vector graphics do not take up a lot of space the file size will be reduced.*
>
> *Overall, vector graphics are appropriate because of the amount of resizing that occurs; the large size of maps requires small file sizes and the probability that photographic quality images will not be required.*

## Discuss

In this example, you need to identify a point and follow it up with reasoned discussion reaching a logical conclusion.

In a good answer you should be looking at different points of view/ sides of the discussion. These should be given as positives/negatives or advantages/disadvantages.

Your essay should end with a conclusion. Make sure you reach a specific conclusion and include phrases such as 'In conclusion…', 'Overall…', 'On balance…'. Your conclusion should be a shortened summary of the main points with a reason for opting for one side over the other.

## Example

**6** Discuss the impact of ICT on air travel.

| Answer | Commentary |
|---|---|
| *For longer flights there is the use of in-flight entertainment such as hand held games, back of the seat entertainment systems and portable music systems. These have had a positive consequence of giving greater passenger satisfaction. This is because passengers will not just be sitting for long periods of time with nothing to do, they will be occupied and their minds will be taken off the fear of flying or the long hours of boredom. Children, in particular, will be better behaved and this will reduce stress and annoyance for other passengers. If passengers are satisfied, they are more likely to fly with that airline in the future, increasing its passenger numbers and overall revenue.* | ▪ Identification of one point that will be discussed<br>▪ Description: in-flight entertainment systems is a vague term – it has been expanded<br>▪ Identification of a positive impact – that of customer satisfaction<br>▪ The reasons why and how in-flight entertainment brings about customer satisfaction<br>▪ This highlights children in particular and starts to tie the impacts to the consequences<br>▪ The paragraph concludes with the consequences to the particular airline |

The answer given above focuses on an impact and its consequences/effects.

It is a good idea to choose one positive and one negative point. Write at least half a side on each point. Do not be tempted to stray and write about different points in the same paragraph. Make sure you give the point, the impacts of the point and the consequences of those impacts. You need to write half a page on each point for a good answer.

If you choose more than two points you are unlikely to have time to fully develop your answer and reach a reasoned conclusion.

Compare the above example with the one below:

*A negative impact of ICT on air travel could be that pilots may not be needed in the future if ICT can control and fly the aircraft itself. This would minimise jobs and deskills humans.*

This answer does not develop the point or go into detail about the impacts. It is a series of statements.

Remember to develop each point and follow it through to its logical conclusion.

# ■ General examination tips

The examination is the end point that all your preparation has been leading up to. You really do need to be prepared, to have put the revision in, looked over past questions and understand how to answer different types of questions. You then stand much more chance of giving answers that will be awarded marks. The following are some techniques that you can use in the examination room to help you get the best out of you.

## Focus on the question you are answering

Forget the last question and the next section question. Concentrate on reading the current question and structuring the best answer you can, making sure to match the keyword and the marking scheme.

## One mark per minute

If a question is worth two marks then do not spend more than two minutes writing the answer. Sometimes candidates' answers go into too much detail. This means that later answers are rushed and marks are lost due to wasted time. The identify/state questions require short and sharp answers – they are usually knowledge focused – so get them out of the way quickly.

## Find a relaxation point

During the examination it is a good idea to give your brain, back and eyes a brief rest. Look at the clock or a point at some distance just to relax for 30 seconds or so. Do not look around the room as this will distract others and interrupt your thought processes. It is also a good idea to alternate between using two different pens with different shapes to help rest your hand as you write for a sustained period.

## No crossing out

No marks are lost for incorrect answers. If an answer has been crossed out it will not get marked if you have written an alternative answer. If you do not cross out the answer then it will be marked and may still get credit. Only cross out an answer if the question is worth one mark as only the first response will be marked. If you do need to cross out anything, then be organised. Use a single line and then calmly write a second answer.

## Always read carefully what you have written

Read through your answers and make sure you have written exactly what you need to say. The words used and their order can make a difference, so take care. You need every mark. Does the examiner need to add anything to your answer to make sense? If so, then you need to add some more. Add one more example in your response if it is appropriate. Take that bit of extra time to think about your answer before you start to write.

# Structured tasks guide

The coursework for OCR AS ICT is worth 40 per cent of the whole AS level. The coursework is structured and it is essential that you have a go at all of the tasks and complete all of the elements within each task.

The structured tasks are based on a requirements list and relate to the given scenario and client, for example a local gymnastics club or a children's hospital. Even if you disagree with a task or think it irrelevant, you need to do what the client asks for. When you complete the tasks, you will need to show evidence of the following skills:

- Design
- Software development
- Testing
- Documentation

## ■ Design

A design should be done either by hand or using a different piece of software from the one that will be used in software development. If the task says done by hand, then you MUST complete it by hand. The information given in the question must be included in the design. The information might ask you to go onto a web page, computerise a data capture form or give you questions that need to be asked. Even if you miss a single piece of information you will lose marks. Read the task carefully and check that you have included all the required information.

A design specification is information about the design – it covers formatting aspects such as the colour, style and size of the font to be used. If you are asked to create a design and a design specification, it is best to create the design on a sheet of A4 paper. Then stick your design into the middle of a sheet of A3 paper and, in the space surrounding your design, write the design specification.

## ■ Software development

This is the creation of the spreadsheet, database, web page or presentation. The only evidence that you give to the moderator is what you print out and submit. You may have created a fantastic system but if you do not provide useful printouts you will not get marks.

When providing evidence make sure that you do not miss anything.

If asked for evidence of formulas all of the function needs to be seen and there should be no truncating. In spreadsheets, row and column headings need to be shown. If named cells are used these should also be shown.

Make sure any screenshots are large enough for the examiner to see.

| =VLOOKUP(K2,$H$1 | =IF(D1="Yes",A |
|---|---|
| =VLOOKUP(K3,$H$1 | =IF(D2="Yes",A |
| =VLOOKUP(K4,$H$1 | =IF(D3="Yes",A |

# ■ Testing

There are two parts to testing – the test plan and the testing itself.

Test plans could cover three main areas:

- **Valid** – normal data that the system should work with.

- **Invalid** – incorrect data that the system should pick up and generate an error message.

- **Extreme** – boundary data on the edge of tolerance.

For example, in a spreadsheet, if you had a cell that should only accept numbers between 1 and 20, there are up to five tests that could be performed on the cell:

| 0 | 1 | 10 | 20 | 21 |
|---|---|---|---|---|
| ↑ | ↑ | ↑ | ↑ | ↑ |
| Invalid lower | Extreme lower | Normal | Upper extreme | Upper invalid |

In the example above, two of the tests will produce error messages. Make sure that you carry out different tests, not just the same one several times, for example five tests with normal data on the same cell.

If you are given a test table in the task make use of it. Make sure you follow the instructions for testing. If you are asked for a certain number of valid/invalid tests make sure you have enough of each.

When producing the output of the tests make sure that the test number on the test plan matches the number of the output.

When you present the results of testing make sure that the data value that was input can be seen and has been labelled. For example:

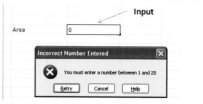

Input value cannot be seen – no marks.

Input value can be seen and has been identified – marks.

## Test plans

When creating a test plan you must make sure you identify the input data and where it is going to go and the output data and where it is to be found. For example:

| Test | Description of test | Type of test | Input data values | Expected output value | |
|------|---------------------|--------------|-------------------|----------------------|---|
| 1 | Change the court hire prices | Valid | Change a price to a new number | The total price will change for a customer | ✗ Too vague |
| 2 | Change the price of unit 2 | Valid | Input £5.50 into cell C3 on the PRICES worksheet | Member 1 who has booked 5 units will be charged £22.50 in cell I2 on the TENNIS worksheet | ✓ All information required |

The philosophy of testing is:

- The text plan should be understood by a third party.
- They should be able to run the test using ONLY the information given.
- The test should be repeatable by a different person.

# ■ Documentation

There are two types of documentation – help sheets and full user documentation.

All the documentation that you create is for a specific purpose and a specific audience. You must bear these two points in mind at all times and ask the question, is the documentation that you are creating 'fit for purpose'?

## Full user documentation

Full user documentation must include all of the following elements:

- Title page
- Contents page (should be automatically generated by the software)
- Introduction/purpose
- Hardware/software to be used
- The guide itself (help sheets on individual aspects)
- Troubleshooting
- Glossary
- Index

The documentation should have page numbers and be presented in a format appropriate to the audience. It should be standalone and completely computerised.

Help sheets should include text and pictures. You need to begin by considering how the application is to be opened and where the file is located. The rest of the help sheet should focus on giving instructions.

Once you have completed the documentation, spell check it and re-read what you have written. Ask a friend to have a go at using it. Finally, has everything been covered in the task that was supposed to be?

# ■ General rules

There are some general rules that you should follow that will help you gain good marks:

- Look at the number of marks available – this will give you an indication of how much work is required.

- Read through the whole of the task and look at whether anything you are doing at the beginning is going to be used later on – this is particularly true of design, software development, test plans and the results of testing.

- When designing, read the task and mark any important pieces of data that you are going to need to include.

- Spell check everything and check it through. Sometimes the spell checker will not pick up a spelling mistake – you may have misspelt a word but accidentally used another word that has been spelt correctly!

- Use the correct software – just because you happen to like a particular piece of software does not mean it is appropriate for the task. Listen to the guidance that your teacher gives you about software selection.

- You must attempt all the tasks and every element included in the task. If you have difficulty with an element, work around the problem – it will not get you marks but will allow you to move onto the rest of the task. For example, if in a spreadsheet there is a formula that is difficult and you cannot do it, type in the answer given by hand. At least the rest of the spreadsheet will work and you can move onto the later elements of the task.

- Presentation is important. Including a cover sheet for every task is very helpful. Make sure to include your name, candidate number, centre name and centre number. Do not submit your work in ring binders or plastic folders – cardboard folders are best, remembering your details on the front cover.

# Keywords index

# Index